P9-ASN-654

BUTLER PUBLIC LIBRARY
BUTLER, PENNSYLVANIA 16001
178 1140

799.2
TRO

The Complete Book of Wild Turkey Hunting

A Handbook of Techniques and Strategies

JOHN TROUT, JR.

THE LYONS PRESS

Copyright © 2000 by John Trout, Jr.

All rights reserved. No part of this book may be reproduced in any man-
ner without the express written consent of the publisher, except in the
case of brief excerpts in critical reviews and articles. All inquiries
should be addressed to: The Lyons Press, 123 West 18 Street, New
York, New York 10011

Printed in Canada

10 9 8 7 6 5 4 3 2 1

Library of Congress Cataloging-in-Publication Data

Trout, John, 1946–
    The complete book of wild turkey hunting: a handbook
of techniques and strategies/John Trout, Jr.
        p. cm.
    ISBN 1-58574-099-3
    1. Turkey hunting—Handbooks, manuals, etc. I. Title.
SK325.T8 T76 2000
799.2'4645—dc21

00-57932

To someone special in my life who loves turkey hunting as much as I . . . my darling wife, Vikki.

Contents

ACKNOWLEDGMENTS

I could not begin to thank everyone who has contributed, one way or another, to the completion of this book. There are those with whom I have hunted over the years, family members, and others who provided the necessary support that made it possible for me to spend time in the field. I also appreciate those editors who have published my writing and photos. I only hope my works have inspired veteran turkey hunters and newcomers alike.

My wife, Vikki, has always supported my writing, photography, and love for the wild turkey. I express special gratitude for her help with proofing the pages that follow. Most important, I have cherished her decision to become a turkey hunter and a hunting buddy.

I am also grateful to my son, John, for the hunting time we have shared. He took his first turkey many years ago, and I was fortunate to be there. Neither of us can begin to state in words the pride we shared.

The individuals who provided interviews for this book sacrificed their valuable time and provided support. Their assistance is greatly appreciated.

Finally, I thank the National Wild Turkey Federation, biologists, and other specialists who have contributed to the successful restoration of the wild turkey. A special thanks to Indiana wild turkey biologist Steve Backs for allowing me to spend time in the field with him and tie him up for hours on the telephone over the years.

PREFACE

If I have learned anything about turkey hunting, it has to be that no two turkeys are alike. Every bird seems to possess a personality of its own, and every bird will respond to a call differently. This book emphasizes the importance of judging every turkey individually and of never taking hunting tactics for granted. I seriously doubt that anyone on the face of this earth knows everything about turkey hunting, or ever will. We may think we do on a given day, only to be ridiculed by a gobbler the next day.

Thirty years ago, it would have been hard to find a book on hunting wild turkeys. In fact, even turkey hunters were hard to come by back then. Most national hunting publications ran a story now and again on the subject, but even they were rare and unlike the magazine articles of today.

The old turkey-hunting stories simply covered the basics. Modern periodicals paint an entirely different picture. Every major hunting publication now makes it a point to run advanced stories about hunting the elusive and majestic turkey. That is understandable, considering there are more turkeys, more turkey-hunting opportunities, and more turkey hunters who crave information about advanced tactics. After all, the more we pursue this great bird, the wiser and more challenging it becomes.

Veteran hunters will find that this book provides the fascinating methods to outsmart the precocious turkey of today, while novice hunters will discover unimaginable secrets. Because this book goes far beyond the basics, it is not just another turkey-hunting book. For instance, many turkey-hunting books include chapters on basic, spring turkey calls and basic hunting techniques. However, since every turkey is a distinct character, there can be no one reliable method, no one particular call that will get the job done each time you bump heads with the wariest of game birds. You must evaluate each turkey before deciding on the method that will lure him into range. The pages that follow do just that, focusing on spring gobblers that do not come waltzing into the first call they hear. There are chapters about calling to birds at sunrise; beating competing hens; hunting gobblers that hang up, afternoon turkeys, and pressured and late-season birds; and many more, including a chapter dedicated to hunting fall turkeys.

The layout of this book is easy to follow and promptly gets into the spring hunt. I could have included more chapters on spring hunting, but the chapters mentioned previously are by far the most important to achieve a successful spring hunt.

You will find the largest chapters early in the book. If you have a love for the wild turkey, and you obviously do if you are reading this introduction, you will not want to overlook "Biology and Behavior," chapter 2, which is loaded with life-cycle facts about turkeys, from poults to adulthood. The more insight you have about the habits of the wild turkey, the better your chances are of tagging a bird.

Another chapter you won't want to miss is found in the latter part of the book. Chapter 18 gives tips for recovering turkeys after the shot. Most hunters do get their birds after the shot, but there is always that one bad day when something goes terribly wrong, and you have to search for a crippled bird. In addition, chapter 19 is about photographing the wild turkey, and hunting experiences. Nearly every hunter, at one time or another, has wished he could make his hunt last forever, or see a certain gobbler just one more time. This chapter includes facts about photography equipment and secrets of photographing the majestic wild turkey.

There are different ways to get points across, particularly when you want to reveal hunting secrets. That is why chapter 16 is devoted to success stories from some of the nation's top spring turkey hunters of how they harvested their toughest birds. While each is in itself a true, enjoyable hunting tale, together they add up to valuable insights on what to do if and when you encounter a similar gobbler.

This turkey-hunting book, or any other for that matter, will not provide the one thing that is absolutely necessary to outsmart a wild turkey. It is called woodsmanship and must accompany you to the field. Woodsmanship is achieved only from hunting experiences. Every time you walk into the turkey woods, regardless of whether you call up and shoot a gobbler, you have made yourself a better woodsman. It is not attained by the books you read, or by listening to turkey-hunting tales. However, this book will take care of the rest of your hunt.

INTRODUCTION

I carefully picked my way through the woods in the pitch dark. Using even a small flashlight was out of the question, as its luminance would have given my approach away to the gobbler I knew was roosted close by. I had put him to bed the evening before, and estimated that he was no more than 100 yards from where I had just parked my truck.

This was the first turkey hunt where I was going to call in my own bird. I had planned this hunt carefully, as I didn't want anything to go wrong. As it turns out, among the many things I learned that morning was that mistakes are part of the game when you're hunting wild turkeys. Without them, the hunt becomes a kill, and that would end the anticipation and challenge of hunting this wily bird.

That morning's hunt ended without me getting the opportunity to pull the trigger. But the lessons I learned that

1

day helped form the foundation for the turkey hunter I would become. From understanding that using a small flashlight would have helped me find a better set-up location, to calling too early, too loud, too often, not being ready when the big gobbler came in and, finally, thinking the hunt was over when he ran off. All were lessons I learned that first day, and over many turkey hunting days afield since then. But not once did any of the school of hard knocks' teachings leave me feeling dejected. Rather, they intensified my desire to hunt these cunning birds more efficiently.

I have become a successful turkey hunter over the years, and have taken birds from east to west. I pride myself on being able to call in even the most stubborn of gobblers. But the real value of my experience is that I know that no matter how good of a hunter you think you are, the wild turkey can still teach you some very humbling lessons, no matter how much experience you have gathered.

There are a few turkey hunters who get past even the wiliest of toms. They're "naturals" at hunting turkeys. They seem to instinctively know where to set up, how softly or loudly to call, what types of vocalizations will work under different conditions, and how to get birds to respond when no one else can. Not only can they weave that type of magic, but they also have become experts in sharing their skills with other hunters—the most important and impressive element in being a master hunter.

John Trout, Jr., is one such hunter. He is truly a master at not only hunting turkeys, but teaching others how to successfully hunt them as well. I'm proud to have him as the hunter chosen to write this book. I will learn from his wisdom and his tactics within the pages to follow, and I'm confident you will, too. Whether you're a novice or veteran, you will benefit from John Trout, Jr.'s years of knowledge and skill. He has compiled his practical advice within this book so that both camps can learn from his turkey hunting experiences. I trust this book will be a valuable and treasured book in your outdoor library. It is in mine.

—*Peter Fiduccia*

CHAPTER 1
THE EARLY DAYS

IN APPRECIATION OF THE WILD TURKEY

The old tom turkey came in over a rise, his colorful tail feathers glistening in the early morning sunlight. It was truly a remarkable sight as he gracefully moved through the hardwoods with his white head bobbing about, looking for friend or foe. Meanwhile, I lay in a logjam trying to stay hidden and calm my rapidly beating heart. It was almost more than I could bear on this spring morning before I had begun to hunt this majestic creature.

That incident occurred twenty-five years ago, but I remember it as though it happened yesterday. The gobbler that I saw that morning is long dead by now, while I live on, hunting him every year, thanks to the inspiration that he provided on that cool morning in March. You see, I was there that day to get a taste of what turkey hunting was all about. There were very few birds in southern Indiana back then, not to mention only a handful of hunters. Just the same, I came to the woods to consider the challenge of turkey hunting a few weeks before the spring season began. While scouting and attempting to decipher turkey sign, I heard the bird gobble just after a nagging crow flew overhead. With nowhere to go except the old logjam, I crawled in and waited to see if he would show. He did, and I was hooked.

By the time the spring turkey season made its debut, I had located no fewer than three turkeys, read every magazine article on the subject of hunting the spring gobbler, and thought I had learned the ins and outs of calling. If only my first customer had cooperated. He gobbled from the roost at dawn, and I moved in and set up against a small maple tree. I called, and he gobbled. He gobbled, and I called again. Then I got up and moved, only to flush the bird into parts unknown. This mistake was only the first of many that would haunt me in the spring seasons that followed. I made many more errors that day, and the next day, and the remainder of the days in that season until I finally found one turkey that was so eager to meet his destiny that he forgave me for every mistake I made.

After nervously tagging my first gobbler, I vowed to pursue this fascinating bird as long as the good Lord would allow. Fortunately, my pursuit continues today. I have seen the flocks throughout North America grow to astonishing numbers and have come to understand the exciting challenge that the wild turkey provides to so many enthusiasts.

Others, however, worshiped the wild turkey long before you and I. Native Americans, homesteaders, and even

Spanish explorers considered the bird to be a godsend. They pursued the turkey consistently and feasted upon the birds whenever they were successful. They didn't consider hunting turkey to be the great challenge we do today, but that is understandable if one considers that they sometimes snared them and shot them with dart guns. The birds of long ago also had few encounters with people, which made them easy targets for those who hunted them.

Once abundant, the native North American wild turkey nearly reached extinction in the 1930s. Shortly after settlers moved west, wild turkey populations began to suffer as vast hardwoods were cleared for timber production and agricultural crops. However, that was only the beginning of problems for this great bird. Since the wild turkey was as tasty then as it is now, unregulated hunting contributed further to its reduction. It is believed that the wild turkey inhabited thirty-nine states and Ontario, Canada, in the 1800s. By 1920, its range had dwindled to just eighteen states.

Just how long the *Meleagris gallopavo* (the Latin name for wild turkey) has been here remains somewhat of a mystery. Fossils indicate it has been here for thousands of years. I won't go into the differences between prehistoric turkeys and those you and I hunt today, but I will say that this great bird once thrived in most of the eastern and southwestern United States before it nearly reached extinction during the past century. In fact, after the damage was completed and just before the turkeys came back, only isolated populations remained in favored areas. Those areas would become the thresholds of life for the wild turkey.

In the 1940s and 1950s, many wildlife agencies first attempted to release pen-reared turkeys. It was soon discovered that the barnyard birds could not survive. However, as those states with remnant populations traded wild turkeys to other states and provinces for game that interested them, the restoration program was born. For instance, state game and fish departments often traded grouse and pheasants for turkeys. Some officials even traded big game animals such as moose for wild turkeys. Once a given state or province stocked turkeys in selected areas and populations began to blossom, officials could then trap and transport their birds to other regions. Modern technology and the use of specially designed traps have made this possible and have contributed greatly to the restoration program.

The biggest surprise of restoration programs in recent years lies in the wild turkey's preferred habitat. Biologists once believed the birds would survive best in vast areas of timber. A few years of survival and expansion soon told a different story, however. Today, wild turkey flocks have flourished where a diversity of habitat exists. That is not to say that birds will thrive in any type of habitat, but the wild turkey has taken hold on the plains and in agricultural areas where little timber exists. Just how much timber is necessary for survival will probably remain a mystery for a while longer. I have hunted the Merriam's subspecies in the plains of South Dakota and found an abundance of birds where little timber existed. Because of their ability to survive in almost any type of habitat, it is safe to assume that the wild turkey is probably more adaptable than any other game bird. Both the ruffed grouse and pheasant have a much narrower range of habitat.

Equally important is the turkey's ability to live in proximity to human beings. The birds even flourish in some areas where humans rule the roost. Many folks living in urban and suburban areas report seeing wild turkeys meandering about. Unfortunately, because acreage diminishes each year as we chop further and further into the countryside, habitat loss could become the turkey's worst enemy.

Trapping and transplanting have been responsible for the turkey's success, but not without help from organizations such as the National Wild Turkey Federation and concerned sportsmen. Hunters have contributed millions of dollars to the preservation of habitat and wild turkey management through the sale of licenses. The 1937 Pittman-Robertson Act put an excise tax on sporting goods and ammunitions, providing money to initiate wildlife recovery programs, including wild turkey restoration projects.

Today, restoration efforts have ended for some states while they continue in others. Although trapping and transplanting have subsided in some areas, officials continue to manage the wild turkey in various ways—from regulated harvests to habitat improvements. Because of all this, the wild turkey now inhabits every state except Alaska. This includes ten states that are outside the wild turkey's ancestral range. Although populations of wild turkey have fluctuated in some states for reasons ranging from weather to habitat loss, they continue to increase overall.

According to population estimates provided by the National Wild Turkey Federation's book *The Wild Turkey Biology & Management*, there were about 3.5 million birds in the United States in 1990. Today, that figure is estimated to be about 5 million. Considering that a 1959 census estimated only 465,809 turkeys in the United States, one can easily see that restoration efforts have been most effective.

Wild turkey populations have flourished in recent years. Today, more than 5 million birds inhabit the continent.

Although Texas has the largest wild turkey population in the United States, with about 600,000, at least a dozen other states have more than 100,000 birds within their boundaries. Even those states with populations under 50,000 offer sportsmen plenty of excitement during spring and fall hunting seasons.

Of the five subspecies of wild turkey, the Eastern is the most abundant. Population estimates indicate that there were about 2.5 million Eastern turkeys in the early 1990s, compared to about 637,000 Rio Grande and 101,000 Merriam's subspecies of turkeys. The Osceola, sometimes referred to as the Florida subspecies, accounted for about 75,000 birds, while only about 150 Gould's existed.

Today, hunters pursue all five subspecies of wild turkey in the United States, Canada, and Mexico. The Eastern subspecies is abundant in the Eastern United States as far west

It was once believed the Eastern wild turkey needed vast areas of timber to survive. In recent years, restoration efforts have indicated they are quite adaptable to various types of habitat, including agricultural areas.

as Oklahoma, and from northern Maine to northern Florida. Easterns have also been introduced in some isolated areas in Ontario, Canada. Merriam's inhabit the western half of the United States, where favored habitat exists, while the swamp-loving Osceola subspecies is found only in Florida. The Rio Grande subspecies is abundant in Texas but ranges as far south as Mexico and as far north as Kansas. Central Mexico is home to most Gould's wild turkeys, though a limited number exist in New Mexico.

Biologically speaking, you can consider each of the five subspecies a different race. Each has geographical preferences, and each has a unique appearance. Only the Osceola and Eastern subspecies are similar in color. Because each subspecies possesses a particular personality, hunting tactics must also vary. Many spring turkey hunters have accepted the challenge of a lifetime: attempting to take the Grand Slam and/or the Royal Slam. Harvesting the Eastern, Merriam's, Osceola, and Rio Grande is considered the Grand Slam, while the Royal Slam includes the Gould's as well.

At one time, a turkey hunter may have found it necessary to travel many miles to hunt. Today, many sportsmen can hunt these noble birds within a short drive of home. When I think about the expansion of the wild turkey's range, I envy those youngsters who are just discovering the challenge of hunting them. They will have opportunities far beyond those I had when it all started.

In beginning this chapter, I could not help but discuss the rarity of bumping into a wild turkey. After all, that's the way it was back then, and that's how many of us discovered a new love. Only yesterday, though, as I sat in a tree stand hunting white-tailed deer, eleven gobblers flew off a nearby roost of white pines and landed a mere forty yards from my hideout. For the next forty-five minutes, I watched as they scratched the leaves and fought for pecking order while a few cautious eyes kept a close lookout for predators. Their sharp, strong social behavior and survival instincts have led me to believe that they, too, have contributed to restoration success.

CHAPTER 2
BIOLOGY AND
BEHAVIOR

FACTS THE HUNTER SHOULD KNOW

Not long ago, few people understood the habits of the wild turkey. Today, research biologists, the National Wild Turkey Federation, and turkey hunters throughout North America are all interested in the biology and behavior of this magnificent bird.

Veteran hunters fully understand that you must possess woodsmanship ability and have some understanding of the wild turkey's habits if you hope to be successful. I agree that success has much to do with outguessing the birds. However, you cannot accomplish this without first knowing what a bird may or may not do when a particular tactic is used. Knowing the turkey's habits, such as the spring mating ritual, as well as the language of hens and gobblers, enables you to be one step ahead of your quarry.

PHYSICAL CHARACTERISTICS

The adult wild turkey (two years old and older) has about five thousand feathers covering its body. Its plumage appears dark, and its legs are about two inches longer than the legs of most domestic turkeys. The feet of an adult gobbler may reach a length of 4½ inches. Average weights of adult birds vary depending upon geographical location. Some of the largest gobblers are found in the agricultural areas of the Midwest. Harvest studies indicate they commonly weigh more than twenty pounds, whereas most adult gobblers in other areas weigh less than twenty pounds. Hunters like to take heavy birds, but the length of the beard and spurs interests them even more.

Most biologists consider the beard of a turkey to be a modified feather, not hair, as some people believe. The bristly beard grows about four to five inches each year, the beard of a young gobbler usually becoming visible by the time it is six months old. Turkeys molt and lose feathers periodically, but the gobbler's beard will stay for life, providing it is not torn away from the breast by a predator, fence, or other interference. Beards do wear from being dragged on the ground, usually after they reach a length of about ten inches. Terrain, height of the turkey, and thickness of the beard all play a role in how quickly it wears.

Multiple beards are not uncommon. As far as I know, the record for multiple beards is eight, from a turkey taken in

Contrary to what many believe, the beard of the wild turkey is not hair. It is actually modified feathers that grow annually until dragging affects growth.

Wisconsin in 1989. However, most multiple-bearded turkeys have two or three beards. A friend of mine took his first turkey in Alabama. It carried five beards, but, like most turkeys with multiple beards, it had only one long beard. When a turkey has multiple beards, it is common for one to be eight or nine inches long while the others are only two to six inches.

Beards are not limited to the males. In fact, biologists claim that about one in twenty hens has a beard. Judging from my sightings while photographing turkeys during late winter and early spring for the past decade, I must agree. When I see groups of fifteen to twenty hens, there is usually at least one bearded lady in the flock.

A gobbler's age is determined by the length of his spurs, found on each leg a few inches above the feet. The spurs are actually bones with a fingernail-like covering. Spurs vary in color from black to white, while some appear almost transparent. The gobbler's spur begins growing just after birth and will reach a length of half an inch by the time the bird nears its first birthday. The spurs of many two-year-old birds will be less than 1 inch, while three-year-old birds may carry spurs that are over an inch long. It's rare for spurs to be longer than 1½ inches, as they, like beards, also wear. The rougher the terrain, the more the spurs will wear. This is one reason the spurs of western turkeys do not grow as long as those of Eastern birds.

There are also abnormalities in spurs, just as there are in beards. In the late 1980s, I shot a Missouri gobbler that had no spurs at all. Each leg was slick and showed no sign of spur growth, even though the bird weighed 23½ pounds and sported an eleven-inch beard.

Males and females have several distinct physical characteristics. The adult gobbler's head and neck are red, white, and blue, while the hen's neck and head are much duller and primarily bluish gray. Many times, when I call in a spring gobbler, the first thing I see is the white head. I have often referred to this sighting as like someone turning on a light bulb in the woods. Another notable feature of the gobbler is the large red caruncles (lumpy portions of flesh at the bottom of the neck), which turn blood red when the bird becomes sexually excited. The hen's caruncles appear pink and are smaller. Feathers of hens and gobblers also differ in color. At a distance, you may notice that the gobbler appears almost black, while a hen appears dark brown.

You can distinguish young birds from adult birds by examining the tail feathers. For instance, the middle tail feathers of the juvenile gobbler (called a jake) are longer than the feathers on each side, which are apparent only when a jake struts. The tail feathers of an adult gobbler are the same length throughout the fan. The red caruncles of a sexually excited jake will also be duller than those of a lovesick adult gobbler and more similar to the pink caruncles of a hen.

COMMON TURKEY TALK

Like most birds, the wild turkey is quite vocal. Sounds that turkeys make can vary in pitch and tone because of the age and sex of the bird. However, each sound has a particular meaning.

The most common turkey talk is the *yelp*. Spring turkey hunters learn the yelp first and foremost, and for good reason. Both hens and gobblers yelp, but during the spring a

Gobblers and hens look nothing alike. The gobbler (bottom) has a white cap on its head while the head of the hen (top) is blue-gray. The red caruncles are also much sharper on the gobbler's neck and head.

Jakes have longer middle tail feathers than adult gobblers. This can be noticed when a jake struts.

hen will often yelp to attract gobblers. A gobbler's yelp is more coarse than that of a hen and is usually only a syllable or two. Hen yelps are normally three or more syllables.

You may hear *tree yelps* during the early morning hours when a hen is roosted. They do not really differ from the standard yelps, except they are not as loud. Many hunters use this hen call first thing in the morning after setting up on a roosted gobbler.

Lost yelps are preferred when a hen attempts to round up the flock, particularly during fall and winter. The rhythm is similar to that of standard yelps but is drawn out into numerous syllables. A hen may also use lost yelps after she flies down from the roost. Fall hunters often rely on lost yelps or the *kee-kee* call after busting a flock, hoping it will bring back a turkey that wants to join up with the others.

The kee-kee, also known as the whistle, is a call commonly used by juveniles, particularly when they are attempting to locate a hen. This high-pitched call usually has three or four syllables and may end with a yelp or two. We often hear this call in the fall and winter, because it is one of the first calls the juveniles learn. Some hunters have even used this call in the spring to lure a gobbler into range.

Clucks can vary in tone and may be subtle or loud, but they are only one syllable. All turkeys cluck, which makes this call a favorite for spring hunters attempting to attract a gobbler. The cluck is social talk, and all turkeys use this sound to get the attention of other turkeys. Clucks are easy calls to master and are particularly effective when gobblers become call shy to standard yelps.

Hens will often *cackle* when they fly up and down from the roost. Spring hunters sometimes use the cackle—a series of loud and rapid high-pitched sounds similar to yelps. The cackle will often get a gobbler's attention, but it is a difficult call to master. A similar and more popular spring call is the *cutt*. It is rapid, high-pitched, and slows a bit at the end of the call. In my opinion, the cutt (which is really a series of aggressive broken yelps) is a much better spring call than the cackle because hens use it on the ground. Many hunters use the cutt to induce an otherwise quiet gobbler to respond. It can be an exceptional locator call, which you will read about in a later chapter.

All turkeys *purr* throughout the year. It means that all is well. The purr is softly spoken and difficult to hear unless you are close to the turkey. Spring and fall hunters use this call but do so with very little volume. Turkeys also use a louder purr when they detect danger. When making this sound, a turkey usually stands still and may cock its head to one side. All turkeys will become alert when they hear this sound.

The *alarm putt* is a call that turkeys use when they spot danger. It is similar to the cluck, except that it is a sharper one-syllable sound. If a hunter attempts to make a cluck and ends up with the alarm putt, however, I'm not so sure it will send a turkey running, since there is little difference between the two calls.

In recent years, spring hunters have come to rely on sounds that simulate turkeys fighting. These are actually aggressive purrs. Gobblers and hens fight throughout the year for various reasons, usually making rapid and continuous purrs in the process. Knight & Hale Game Calls introduced the first call to simulate a fighting purr. Today, just about every call manufacturer offers such a device.

I have not discussed every turkey sound that has ever been recorded, but I have focused on those that will have the most influence during hunting seasons. If you have trouble imitating these sounds, I suggest you visit someone who has barnyard turkeys, watch videos and outdoor shows on TV, or buy some cassettes from call manufacturers. The following chapter will also assist you when deciding which turkey calls to purchase.

THE MATING SEASON

Only a turkey hunter fully appreciates the ritual that occurs every spring in the turkey woods. You might witness this truly phenomenal show if you are in the right location. You could also say that the mating period is the foundation of a spring turkey hunt.

Gobblers flock together in the fall months but go their separate ways as spring approaches. Two or three often remain together, while the jakes leave the hens and travel together. The competition also begins among hens. They want to breed, nest, and have little turkeys and will often go to any extreme to get to a gobbler before another hen reaches him.

Most deer hunters know that the whitetail rut is triggered by decreasing sunlight in autumn. Increasing daylight during spring triggers the mating season of the wild turkey. Cold temperatures may delay breeding activity, but major gobbling and strutting usually occurs before the spring hunting season starts. Game and fish departments schedule the opening of hunting season about the time hens begin nesting, or when the gobbling peaks.

Gobblers establish a pecking order as mating time nears. Even when two or more adult gobblers are together, one will be dominant and do the breeding. After a gobbler breeds a hen, he wastes no time looking for another mate. He has nothing to do with nesting and rearing young.

When an adult bird gobbles, he fully expects the hen to come to him. The spring turkey hunter attempts to change the law of nature and entice the gobbler to come to the hen instead. Just how often an adult bird will gobble varies. It depends on the number of available hens and how readily the gobbling bird attracts them. However, some jakes will also gobble. Unlike the adult bird's *gobble-obble-obble,* the juvenile gobble is usually broken and disoriented. That is not to say that jakes cannot gobble perfectly. Some can and have fooled veteran hunters, including myself.

A gobbler may gobble at any time of year, but he is especially inclined to do so during spring, particularly when

Gobbling peaks twice during the mating season—once when the mating is about to begin, and again when the hens begin nesting.

weather conditions are favorable. I have heard turkeys gobble to crow calls and other sounds during fall and winter. When a turkey gobbles to any sound it happens to hear, such as a slamming car door, it is referred to as *shock gobbling*. Of course, they may gobble for no apparent reason. Two years before this book got underway, I heard a turkey gobble thirteen times while I was sitting in a tree stand deer hunting on Thanksgiving morning. No sounds provoked the bird to gobble, and I assume it was just his nature to talk whenever he felt like doing so. I have noticed there is less gobbling during the late summer than at any other time of the year.

A second gobbling peak occurs when many hens begin nesting. You could compare this period to the post-rut of the white-tailed buck. The primary breeding has ended, but the bucks make one last effort. The second gobbling peak usually occurs during the late spring season. It is as aggressive as or more aggressive than the first gobbling peak and offers hunters the best opportunity to lure in a gobbler. A turkey will gobble better to locator calls and other sounds during this second peak gobbling period.

During the peak gobbling days, adult birds usually begin talking fiercely at first light while they are still on the roost. Shortly after flying down, a bird may gobble intensely if he hasn't located a hen. Most gobbling subsides as the morning progresses, but a bird may begin gobbling again during the late morning hours. Birds gobble the least during the warmest part of the day. Gobbling may intensify as roost time nears or when birds fly up to roost.

When they are with hens, or when they just feel like it, gobblers strut. This sexually stimulated activity occurs dur-

Spitting and drumming are often heard when a gobbler struts. An observant hunter may hear these sounds up to 75 yards away when favorable conditions exist.

ing all hours of the day, including when they are on the roost at dawn and dusk. The strutting display is unmistakable, as the gobbler drops his wings to the ground, raises his tail feathers, and expands his breast. *Drumming* and *spitting* may be heard when a gobbler struts. You can hear the humming sound of the drum when conditions are favorable and a gobbler is close. I have heard a gobbler drum as far as seventy-five yards away when hunting in quiet woods. Many times, I have known a gobbler was coming into my calls only because I heard him drumming and spitting. The spit is a sharp *fssssst* that precedes the drum.

I often see gobblers masturbating in early spring when I am photographing turkeys. They frequently do it shortly after joining up with hens.

When a hen is ready to breed, she will drop to the ground. The gobbler mounts her from the rear and steps up

It is believed that most mating occurs during midmorning hours. Copulation usually takes only seconds providing the turkeys are left undisturbed.

Hens select cutover areas, fields, logjams, and thickets to lay their eggs. The clutch of eggs is then covered with leaves and debris.

on her back. He may also move his feet up and down, as if he were walking without going anywhere. The hen raises her tail feathers, and copulation occurs quickly. When the mating session ends, the gobbler dismounts and the hen stands up and shakes her body rapidly from side to side.

The time of day when a hen is most likely to breed can vary. From my observations, most breeding takes place about two hours after flydown in the morning.

NESTING AND INCUBATION

Hens often begin looking for a nesting site away from their winter range several weeks before they begin laying eggs. A hen will construct her nest on the ground in a concealed area. Fallen trees, dense brush, cutover areas, and fence lines are often selected as nest sites. She may cover her eggs with small twigs, leaves, vines, and grass as necessary.

Hens commonly lay one egg per day, but it appears there is no rule. Some biologists have noted them laying two eggs on a given day, and some have said they will skip a day. Most hens will lay the entire clutch in about ten to fifteen days. Before and after laying, a hen will feed and move about just as a hen that is not nesting would do. She will roost within a short distance of the nest, however.

Most clutches consist of about twelve eggs. The hen will turn her eggs occasionally and will talk to the upcoming arrivals. Once incubating begins, the hen will usually sleep

When a poult hatches, it makes a fairly even cut around the large end of the egg. When a predator finds a nest, it will make a shamble of the eggs.

on the nest and will not flush unless necessary. During incubation, she may leave the nest to feed periodically. If a predator destroys the nest, she may breed and nest again in a different location.

The incubation period is about twenty-six to twenty-eight days. Two or three days prior to hatching, the poults begin making noises. The hen also begins talking to the poults frequently. Each poult uses an *egg tooth* to make a small hole in the egg. It then begins the *pipping* process, a stage in which it cracks the shell somewhat evenly around the large end of the egg. I have observed that pipping can take several hours and that the poults will take resting periods. No one knows which egg hatches first, the first or the last laid, but the entire hatching process may take up to eighteen hours. Once the poult hatches, the shell is left in two pieces. Each piece is neatly broken, unlike the scattered egg fragments you find when predators destroy a nest.

POULTS AND SURVIVAL

The poults and the hen usually leave the nest within twenty-four hours after the last egg hatches. Feeding is of importance for the poults. They leave not only to begin feeding, but to prevent predators from finding them. Before leaving the nest, *imprinting* occurs. Imprinting is a process of social bonding that poults undergo to recognize the hen's vocabulary. They will then respond to her commands, leave the nest, and never return.

I once hatched some domestic turkeys, which imprinted on me. They primarily paid attention to my voice, which was the first sound they heard during and after hatching. When the poults were only a few days old, my wife called me at work and asked that I come home and tend to the poults. Shortly after I had left them earlier that morning, they had begun calling for me with kee-kee whistles. Nothing she said or did could calm them. Moments after I arrived and talked with them, they calmed down and began purring.

The poults will spend the first couple of weeks on the ground under the wings of the hen, even though they can fly one week after hatching. During this period, the poults will peep constantly, preen, dust, and feed, but they rely heavily on their mother for warmth. Within fourteen to twenty days the poults will be able to roost in the trees with the hen. Biologists have determined that this factor is weather dependent. Cold temperatures may delay how quickly the birds begin roosting. Nonetheless, by the time the poults are roosting, they will have a complex vocabulary.

The poults also establish a pecking order, although that may change. As the birds get older, their range increases, as do the types of food they eat. Poults must have foods that are high in protein, such as grasshoppers and beetles. Insects are often plentiful in fields, but poults are preyed upon by hawks and other predators when they are out in the open and exposed. For this reason, many biologists attempt to manage preferred habitat.

Indiana research biologist Steve Backs showed me how he collects bug samples in given areas to determine how much high-protein food would be available to poults—and adult turkeys, for that matter. He collects his samples with large nets that he uses with a sweeping

Hens often take their poults to fields to locate insects, a much-needed high-protein food for young turkeys.

Indiana wild turkey biologist Steve Backs collects bug samples in a "burn area" to determine the number of invertebrates available to turkeys.

back-and-forth motion. Backs also showed me fields where markers were set up to determine the height of the vegetation. He noted that an ideal field has existing vegetation about ten to twelve inches tall and single stems three to four inches tall that grow under the higher vegetation. When these conditions exist, predators such as hawks may not see the poults. The hen, meanwhile, is able to periscope above the tallest vegetation and see any approaching predator.

Many states select small land parcels for turkey habitat, and burn the dense vegetative growth. The new plants that grow after the burn provide food for herbivores and attract numerous insects for turkeys.

By autumn, the poults have evolved into young turkeys. As the availability of vegetation and insects dwindles, the birds start to feed on acorns and other mast foods.

BEHAVIOR AND HABITS

Other than breeding, feeding is the chief priority after turkeys leave the roost around sunrise. They feed upon a variety of seasonal foods and probably try anything new when the opportunity arises. In spring and summer, they commonly feed on grasses, leaves, and plants; berries such as huckleberry, mulberry, and blackberry; insects; and agricultural crops. During fall and winter, dogwood, grasses, acorns, beechnuts, agricultural foods, persimmons, and other fruits become a staple portion of the turkey's diet. Feeding habits vary geographically and include many more foods than those mentioned here.

Turkeys do not always scratch for food. Whenever possible, they will stretch their necks and peck seeds, berries, insects, and a variety of other foods. They will also jump up and grab what they can. Scratching occurs during every season but is often more prominent during fall and winter when leaves cover food sources.

Examining a scratched area to determine the direction in which a turkey is traveling is seldom easy. Looking at one end of a scratched area for piled leaves doesn't really do any good because turkeys can face any direction when they scratch. However, you can examine a large area and follow scratchings just to know they went from point A to point B. Hunters also can check for scratched areas daily to see how often turkeys are passing through. When food is available, turkeys will not hesitate to return to the same scratched location consistently. You may also hear turkeys scratching. The drier the leaves, the farther you can hear them on a calm day.

Biologists seldom examine droppings when determining what a turkey eats. Instead, they inspect the contents of the crop and the gizzard. Hunters often look at the crop as well to see what a turkey has eaten, primarily because the food is swallowed whole and intact. Digestive processes begin in the gizzard, not the crop.

Water is also required, but turkeys don't always visit water sources to get what they need. They are able to get moisture from morning dew and some plants as well. If there is a shortage of water, however, they may visit a water hole daily. When hunting in Texas, I have found it worthwhile to hunt near water holes, especially in the afternoon.

After feeding the first three or four hours of the morning, turkeys will rest and preen their feathers. Many will lie down on their breast when resting but remain alert. Midday and early afternoon are also prime times for *dusting,* in which turkeys saturate their feathers with loose soil to remove parasites. They usually select sandy areas, dry hills, and even ant mounds to do this. After resting and dusting, the turkeys begin moving and feeding to prepare for roosting.

Just how far does a turkey travel in an average day? Some biologists claim the home range of most turkeys is one to two miles. This may vary from fifty acres to five miles, depending on the terrain and the subspecies of turkey. Home ranges can also change with the season. Unlike ducks and other birds, turkeys do not migrate.

Turkeys will fly up to roost around sunset. Weather may have some bearing on which roost sites birds select. Turkeys do not usually roost in dead trees, and they seem to prefer large hardwoods and pines. Dead trees offer little cover and are unstable, while hardwoods and pines offer both security and cover. Turkeys will usually roost along the side of a hill or in a valley, probably for added protection from bad weather. They may also roost over water, although their reasoning for this has never been fully understood. I would speculate that they might feel there is less chance of a predator getting to them. Once turkeys fly up to roost, they will change limbs a number of times. You can hear the accompanying racket at long distances when conditions are favorable. They hang on by wrapping their feet around a limb, and when they sleep, they face into the wind and tuck their head under a wing.

SURVIVAL

The turkey is a social creature, depending on flock members to detect danger. Any alarm putt will promptly grab the attention of all the birds in a flock. I have noticed that false alarms occur quite often. If the flock does not detect danger after an alarm, however, the birds calm down quickly and go back to feeding.

Eyesight is the turkey's keenest sense. It is probably no better than ours, but their eyes sit neatly on the sides of their head, giving them greater peripheral vision. Turkeys can also see color. However, I have found that bright colors do not cause alarm unless they move. Once, while photographing turkeys, I placed an orange hat on a hen decoy. Several

Turkeys can see color; but if it does not move, it will not alarm them.

birds approached the decoy but paid no attention to it. This is understandable. If one stops to think about the woods where the turkey resides, one realizes that there are bright colors everywhere. On the other hand, see what happens if the bright color suddenly moves.

Turkeys do not have a curious bone in their body. Unlike other creatures—deer, for example, will often make it a point to investigate something they cannot positively identify—turkeys will leave without asking questions whenever they are frightened. Veteran hunters fully understand this fact and are aware that a wild turkey does not tolerate movement if it can't identify the source.

Hunters have said that no one would ever kill a wild turkey if the birds had a good sense of smell. Fortunately, their sense of smell is no better than our own, and their hearing is probably only slightly better than ours. Once a turkey does detect danger, however, it can run fifteen mph and fly up to fifty-five mph.

I do not believe that we can classify the wild turkey as an "intelligent" animal. Let's face it, it has a brain that is close to the size of a walnut. However, its finely tuned survival instincts cause it to appear intelligent. The turkey's wild nature contributes to its ability to be a strong survivor.

CHAPTER 3
GEARING UP

GUNS, BOWS, CALLS, AND MORE

I seriously doubt that any sport requires more gear than
turkey hunting. While it may be true that you need special-
ized equipment regardless of what you hunt, turkey hunters
have found that proper tools are vital to their success. The
wild turkey is North America's largest game bird and one of
the most cunning creatures you can pursue. Killing a wild
turkey requires the best from you and your equipment.

SHOTGUNS AND LOADS

Turkey hunters get the most satisfaction from calling a
turkey into gun range. Squeezing the trigger and killing the

41

turkey is secondary, and the easiest part of your hunt. Getting him into range is what turkey hunting is all about. Instinct then takes over, and you shoot when the proper moment arrives. If all goes well, you pick up your bird and head out of the woods with all the personal pride you deserve.

Unfortunately, many of us work hard to get a bird into range only to blow it at the sound of the buzzer. The first two turkeys I shot at did not come out of the woods over my shoulder. I was inexperienced and carried my favorite squirrel gun into the turkey woods. It was a 12-gauge, full-choke and did a fair job of holding a pattern when shooting light 2¾-inch loads. After missing one bird and crippling another, however, I wised up and got a true turkey gun.

Although some states allow the use of centerfire rifles, there is little sense in discussing these guns since most hunters prefer calling turkeys into close range and shooting them with a trusty shotgun. Today, many gun manufacturers produce shotguns designed specifically for turkey hunting. That is not to say that the shotgun in your gun cabinet may not be the perfect turkey gun. Many of the old, full-choke shotguns can produce a tight pattern up to forty yards. Make certain you camouflage your gun before hunting, however. Many manufacturers offer camo paint and tape for making your gun invisible.

Before further discussing shotguns and loads, let me first say a few words about shooting a turkey with a shotgun. The wild turkey is not an animal that should be body-shot. They are tough birds and their feathers can absorb shot. A tight pattern that strikes a turkey in the body at less than twenty yards may get the job done, but many times a body shot will result in a crippled bird. For this reason, shoot only at the neck and head of the turkey. At a reasonable distance, the shot will penetrate into the vitals of the bird's head and neck, dropping him immediately.

Since your shotgun must be able to shoot a tight pattern up to thirty or forty yards, I suggest you stick with a full-choke barrel. Many of today's turkey guns also offer an extra-full choke. This is beneficial if your full choke does not pattern effectively.

Although you could choose a side-by-side or double barrel, you should consider that those guns weigh more than a single-barrel shotgun. As many turkey hunters know, you often find yourself holding up a shotgun for more than a few seconds. This weight can stack up heavily on your arms when you're waiting for the right opportunity to squeeze the trigger.

I would go as far as saying that the most popular turkey shotgun today is a 12-gauge with a three-inch chamber. The big 10-gauge has gained in popularity in recent years, but many hunters, including me, do not like the extra weight of the 10-gauge. My favorite gun today is the Winchester Model 1300. Its short barrel and extra-full choke shoot tight up to forty yards. More about distance and loads in just a moment.

Many modern turkey guns are suited perfectly for women and children. They are available in 16- and 20-gauge and are shorter and lighter. The distance at which they pattern effectively may decrease when compared to the 12-gauge, however. Another possibility is modifying a shotgun to suit the shooter. For instance, my wife currently uses a Remington Model 870 Turkey Express. This 12-

gauge gun was a bit long at first, but we had the stock short-ened by a quality gunsmith and now it fits her perfectly. Barrels can also be shortened if necessary. In fact, 28- and 30-inch barrels are not necessary for turkey hunting, since you don't normally have to worry about swinging and lin-ing up on a flying bird, as a duck or goose hunter does.

Choosing the right load is just as important as selecting the right shotgun. At one time, hunters backed up their No. 4s or 6s with No. 2s. Today, many states have outlawed No. 2s. Other hunters choose to hunt with No. 5s. Most turkey hunters prefer No. 4, 5, or 6 shot, while a few insist upon No. 7½ shot. However, when choosing the right size shot, be aware that not all shot sizes will pattern the same in all guns. For example, your No. 4 shot might pattern tightly up to thirty-five yards in your gun, whereas it will not pattern

The author uses a Lohman Sight Vise to pattern his turkey gun.   (Credit: Vikki Trout)

tightly in your buddy's shotgun. The copper-plated buffered loads have certainly made it more possible to shoot tight patterns, however, and I would recommend using those loads.

I have come to rely on three-inch loads of No. 6 shot for various reasons. For one, I like the idea of getting more than four hundred pellets in a two-ounce load of No. 6 shot, compared to getting fewer than three hundred pellets in a two-ounce load of No. 4 shot. But keep in mind that many hunters choose the No. 4 shot because it may penetrate brush better than No. 6 shot. Distance has not been a problem for me with No. 6s. Though I seldom shoot from more than forty yards, I have killed turkeys at longer distances.

Try different shot sizes to see which load patterns best. What works for one gun may not be best for another.

NUMBER OF PELLETS IN POPULAR
SHOT SIZES AND LOADS.

Lead Shot Size	Number of Pellets in 1-oz. load	Number of Pellets in 1⅛-oz. load	Number of Pellets in 2-oz. load	Number of Pellets in 2¼-oz. load
No. 4	135	253	270	304
No. 5	170	319	340	383
No. 6	225	422	450	450

Several years ago, a bird I was hunting held his ground and refused to move at a distance I estimated to be about forty-five yards away. Knowing that was close to my effective shooting range, I squeezed the trigger. The bird dropped, and I was ecstatic. After walking off the distance, I discovered the turkey had hung up at forty-seven yards. I do not use this as an excuse to shoot farther than forty yards, but I will do that if the bird holds perfectly still, if brush will not deflect my shot, and if he refuses to come closer. In my opinion, even a big 10-gauge loaded with 3½-inch shells should not be an excuse for shooting farther than forty-five yards.

There is something else to consider after you have found the right loads and shotgun. First, and most important, your shotgun and loads must get the job done in the field. I have used a 12-gauge pump shotgun chambered with three-inch No. 6 copper-plated buffered shot for many years. It works. As the old saying goes, "If it ain't broke, don't fix it."

SIGHTS

There are a few different options when choosing sights for your shotgun. You can consider a scope, the standard

Using a telescopic sight is not necessarily better than the traditional bead on the barrel, or the newer fiber-optic sights. Some hunters swear by scopes while others claim they make it difficult to pick up a target.

ribbed barrel with beads on the barrel, or perhaps the newer fiber-optic sights.

More telescopic sights are used today than ever before. If you want to use telescopic sights, I would suggest that you invest in a low-powered scope such as a 2X to 4X. This will increase your chances of finding the bird in low light and in brush. A scope with a large center reticle is also recommended, since you cannot easily see thin crosshairs.

I do not use a scope, primarily because I shoot less than forty-five yards most of the time and can easily find the white head of a turkey in brush by using open sights. Other hunters may argue that telescopic sights are better. Eyesight is another factor. Hunters with vision problems may find it more difficult to find their target when using open sights.

Although many of us feel comfortable using a ribbed barrel with only a white or gold front sight, the new fiber-optic sight may offer an advantage. This adjustable sight is highly visible and can be installed as a front sight only, or as a front and rear sight. The only drawback to the front and rear sight is that you must align the two sights the same when hunting as you did when you sighted-in your gun. Of course, the same could be said for using only a front sight. I would wager that most missed shots with open sights occur because the hunter shot over the bird.

ARCHERY EQUIPMENT

I have been an avid bowhunter for more than thirty-five years. However, for obvious reasons I have not made a habit of pursuing the wild turkey with bow and arrow. I will say, though, that when I have done it, the challenge is incredible. I first hunted the Rio Grande turkey in Texas with bow and arrow but only after taking my first bird with a shotgun. It was fun. On one occasion, three gobblers came to within twelve yards of my ambush location. I could not draw the bow without the turkeys seeing me and could only watch as they walked back into the mesquite from where they had come. After two days of trying to get a gobbler into bow range, I managed to lure a bird to within twenty-five yards only to shoot under him.

I have found that equipment is not necessarily the most important aspect of archery hunting. The most difficult part of hunting the wild turkey with bow and arrow is getting off the shot. For this reason, you may in fact need to modify your equipment to make it easier to shoot a turkey.

If you decide to hunt turkeys with a bow, you are probably a seasoned bowhunter and should consider using the same bow that you use to hunt deer or any other species. The only drawback is the weight of your bow or the weight you pull.

Many modern bows now weigh four pounds or less. These are ideal, since you might find yourself holding for a long time when waiting for a turkey to walk into range. Let-off is another factor to consider. If you do not insist on using traditional equipment, you might want to try a bow with a let-off of 75 percent or more. I use a bow with a 65 percent let-off but go one step further and reduce my pulling weight. When hunting big game, I normally hold about sixty-three pounds. When turkey hunting, I prefer to hold only about fifty pounds, simply because I know that it may be necessary to hold for a long time.

You should also match your arrows with your pulling weight. If you do not change anything, you should stay with the same-weight arrows you use when hunting other animals. However, if you decrease your pulling weight, you will probably need a lighter arrow.

The best broadhead is one that is razor sharp. Many years ago, some archers felt it best to use a broadhead with a washer installed between the end of the arrow and the broadhead. The idea of the washer was to keep the arrow from penetrating totally. Today, most bowhunters realize that it is better to penetrate and not risk poor arrow flight because of the washer. In fact, the ideal setup is probably a sharp broadhead that flies like a field point and has a minimum cutting diameter of 1¼ inches.

You should also make certain that your bow and accessories are quiet and camouflaged. Add moleskin to your arrow rest and plunger if necessary, as well as to any parts of your bow that an arrow could touch.

Bowhunters often use small stools so they can be more comfortable. Some archers prefer to kneel when shooting at a turkey. Either way, most will use a camo netting blind, hide securely in a logjam or brush, or get on the back side of a big tree. The best method when shotgun hunting is to sit on the front side of a big tree, but this can spoil a shooting opportunity for a bowhunter. So some get on the back side

Bowhunters often use camo blinds but only when opportunity allows. When you need to set up quickly, consider a logjam, thicket, or the back side of a large tree.

of a tree, watch for the turkey to approach, and draw the bow when they cannot be seen.

Unlike the shotgun hunter, who shoots for the head and neck, the bowhunter shoots for the heart and lungs. Unfortunately, that target is about the size of a Jonathan apple. For that reason, you must know precisely where the heart and lungs are located on a turkey and take only those shots within your effective shooting range.

TURKEY CALLS

My first turkey call was a Lynch box. I used it extensively the first couple of years I hunted. Many other hunters also start out with a box call, and for good reason. It sounds like the real thing, and it is easy to use. However, I would never consider heading for the turkey woods with only one box call today. In fact, I rely on various types of friction calls and mouth diaphragms.

Perfect turkey calling is not necessary for success. However, you do have to sound something like a turkey. I have had gobblers respond to bad calls, and I have had them shut down entirely when I have made the sweetest sounds any gobbler would want to hear. Even hens sound different. Some produce raspy sounds while others produce high-pitched sounds. The first key is rhythm and to come back with a good call if you make a bad one. Second, you should never rely on one turkey sound to call up a bird. That is why I did not choose to write a chapter on calling turkeys. You simply cannot discuss any right or wrong way to call turkeys when the personalities of the birds differ so much. However, later chapters will discuss the types of birds you will face and the calling strategies that work best.

There are various friction calls to choose from. The box call is the oldest type of friction call, and it produces many effective turkey sounds. When you strike the hinged lid against the lower chamber of the box, you can effectively produce yelps, clucks, and purrs. With practice, you can also get aggressive and make cutts. Push-button box calls have added a new dimension in turkey calls and require less practice. However, they cannot provide as much volume as traditional box calls. One new call that produces more volume than the push-button box yet is as easy to use is the Pump-Action Yelper, manufactured by Lohman. The call is hand-operated and incorporates a mouth diaphragm.

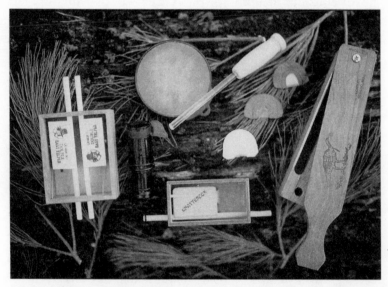

It is not hard to find turkey calls that are easy to master and produce authentic sounds. However, always carry several types of calls so you can vary pitch, tone, and volume as necessary.

There are times when more volume is better. Slate, glass and wood friction calls sound very much like a turkey and remain popular with hunters. Nonetheless, they cannot supply volume like aluminum friction calls. Aluminum friction calls produce high-frequency sounds that can rattle the woods when volume is necessary.

Slate, glass and aluminum friction calls work by running a striker across the surface of the call. One drawback is moisture, which can play havoc on the sounds you produce. For this reason, you might consider one of the new strikers whose manufacturers claim they will work when wet. Woods Wise Products recently introduced the Never Stick–Mystic Stick. It will strike firmly even when oil is on the surface of the call, allowing the hunter to gain volume when needed.

Another drawback to friction calls is that they require two hands to operate. Mouth diaphragms are much more difficult to master than friction calls, but they do keep your hands free to take care of other important business. Mouth diaphragms come with any number of reeds. Those with three or four reeds may be more difficult to use, but they are hard to beat for producing yelps, clucks, and cutts. Single- and double-reed diaphragms are better when you want to produce purrs and kee-kee calls.

Not everyone's palette is suitable for blowing a mouth diaphragm. I am fortunate, in that I can use most any brand and produce authentic turkey sounds, but this did not come easily. Some are harder to master than others, and I have found that two of the same calls made by the same manufacturer may differ in tone and pitch. Diaphragms are not expensive, so it is worthwhile to invest in several to see which is easiest for you to use.

I would also suggest that you try the split-reed mouth diaphragms. In my opinion, those calls make it easier to produce sharper sounds, stay in rhythm, and break each yelp into crisp syllables. The split-reed diaphragms also make the best cutting calls.

You will find that your mouth diaphragms will last longer if you keep them clean and free of moisture. Flush them occasionally and dry them before storing. After using a diaphragm in the field, I blow air between the reeds before storing it.

You can also consider other mouth calls that require suction. Wingbone and tube calls are more difficult to use than mouth diaphragms, but hunters who have mastered them seem to swear by them. Tube calls are excellent calls when you need volume. Wingbone calls have been around for eons and can produce great yelps. Call collectors love to get their hands on original wingbone calls.

How many turkey calls should you take into the field? Spring hunters should consider several, while fall hunters may need only a call that produces yelps, clucks, and kee-kees. When hunting in spring, I usually take a box call and an aluminum friction call for extra volume. I may also take a slate call for close-up encounters where subtle purrs and clucks are necessary. Finally, I carry no less than three mouth diaphragms.

It is important that you have enough calls to produce any pitch and tone. For instance, a gobbler may respond to a raspy sound on one day but answer only a high-pitched sound on another day. He may respond to aggressive hen talk one day and prefer gentle love talk on another. The hunter should have a variety of calls to be able to give a bird what he wants to hear.

Another factor is the type of call used. A wooden box call sounds different than any type of friction call that uses a striker, and a mouth diaphragm sounds different than any friction call. I have found that birds also prefer different calls geographically. In one area, they may love your diaphragm; in another area, they may respond only to a friction call.

LOCATOR CALLS

Locater calls are calls you use to simulate sounds of birds or mammals. Obviously, you must first locate a bird before you can call him into range. The locator call is just the thing to make something happen when nothing else works. Many birds will shock-gobble to some locator calls, while others will gobble to almost any sound.

You can choose from a variety of locator calls. Manufacturers continue to create new ones, and there is always something different to try. Owl hooters and crow calls started the locator-call revolution, but today some hunters commonly use peacock screamers, hawk whistles, and woodpecker calls. Some use duck and goose calls and even coyote howlers. In fact, coyote howlers have been very effective for me when hunting the Merriam's subspecies in South Dakota.

It would be difficult to say which locator call is best. However, I do know that you must use any locator call wisely to achieve results. Owl hooters always seem to work better during the early spring season. This may be because

The author uses a locator call to find a gobbler. A locator call may make a bird gobble when sweet hen talk fails to get a response.

they become overused as the season progresses. Crow calls are probably my favorite, but I believe in using them aggressively. You can easily simulate the sounds of fighting crows to get a gobbler fired up.

A locator call serves two purposes: 1) it can make a gobbler talk when he is in the mood to gobble; 2) it can make a gobbler talk when he is not in the mood to gobble. However, locator calls must be used at the right times. I would not suggest you begin using a locator call long before dawn, even if it is an owl hooter. First, give the birds a chance to talk on their own. If they do not gobble, then you can resort to a locator call before leaving the area.

To achieve the best results, use the right locator call at the right time of day. For example, once you hear crows getting lively, your crow call may work. The crow call may be effective anytime during the day. Use other locator calls, such as duck and goose calls and coyote howlers, during the early morning and late afternoon hours when those critters talk most.

When you use a locator call the first time, do so with little volume in case a gobbler is close. Increase the volume if you do not get a response. Finally, do not limit yourself to only those locator calls that fit the area. You can use a peacock screamer even if there are no peacocks in the area. The right turkey may gobble to any sound, including thunder, gunshots, or a horse that serenades the countryside.

The key to using locator calls is to be versatile and use those capable of producing volume. They are not hard to master, and they are inexpensive. Thus, I would suggest you not be afraid to try several when afield. That one certain locator call may work when another does not.

DECOYS

Regardless of whether you hunt with bow or gun, a decoy may help, because the turkey might focus its attention on the simulated turkey instead of on you and your calls. However, be aware that there is a time and place for using decoys. You may also find that some brands are better than others. Before using a decoy, first check the regulations where you plan to hunt, as they might be illegal.

Though I seldom use decoys, I have killed turkeys in the spring using them. Heck, I remember one gobbler that came into a Flambeau full-body hen decoy a few years ago. He would have mounted her had his lights not gone out first.

Hen decoys are excellent tools for attracting hens that are with gobblers. Some hens that want to breed will pick a fight with a new girl, or will simply want to check her out. Gobblers may also respond to hen decoys, but they may be more interested in picking a fight with another gobbler. For this reason, many decoy manufacturers have introduced jake decoys. The new half-strut jake decoys have become very popular in recent years. Any jake decoy could work, but one in the half-strut position could appear as a threat to an adult gobbler's masculinity. Some hunters will even place a half-strut jake decoy with hens when attempting to attract a spring gobbler.

Safety is a major factor when using turkey decoys. Always make certain you place them in an open area where you can see another hunter approaching, but not directly in front of your ambush location if you could be in the line of fire.

Remember that decoys should not become an excuse to put less time into perfecting woodsmanship and calling

Turkey decoys may attract a spring gobbler but your woodsmanship ability will play the biggest role in your success.

ability. Those factors kill far more turkeys than decoys. Also, setting up a decoy takes valuable time. Since you need to place decoys strategically, I recommend using them only when time allows.

CLOTHING AND ACCESSORIES

There is no such thing as having too many pockets. Perhaps that is why the camo turkey hunter's vest became so popular. I am not sure who introduced this item, but I'm grateful someone did. Many vests now come with pockets specially designed for friction calls, mouth diaphragms, and water bottles. A vest makes it easy to keep everything

Consider wearing a turkey hunter's vest to keep your calls and accessories organized.

organized, allowing you to find a particular gadget at a moment's notice. Most are equipped with a seat that can be lowered promptly, and a pouch for packing out your turkey.

The turkey hunter should also consider a variety of other paraphernalia to store in his vest. You should have a knife, compass, water bottle, and food if you plan to spend several hours afield, as well as insect repellent, a fold-up rain jacket, and extra shotgun shells or archery gear. A small flashlight may be needed, as is emery cloth and chalk to clean and improve the sound of friction calls. Binoculars will come in handy if you are hunting in open areas. You might also want to carry a blaze-orange handkerchief or sock hat.

Turkey hunters can count on covering a lot of ground. A lightweight, waterproof boot with ankle support will make it possible for you to do so without undue stress. Boots that serve you well when you're hunting other game may not be well suited for turkey hunting. One new boot manufactured by Herman Survivors is designed with the turkey hunter in mind. The Turkey Master is available in a 6- and 8-inch boot and has all of the above features, plus a "Bob" sole to enhance traction. Other fine lightweight turkey hunting boots include Rocky's WildCat, and Danner's Fantail.

Turkey hunters know how important it is to wear suitable camouflage. I prefer brushed cotton because it is quiet. You will also need a face mask and gloves. Make certain the face mask does not obstruct your vision and wear gloves that do not hinder your ability to feel your equipment and shoot effectively.

CHAPTER 4
PRESEASON
STRATEGIES

THE FIRST STEP OF A SUCCESSFUL SPRING HUNT

Some of the best spring turkey hunters are those who begin working at it long before the season begins. Many of those people started hunting in states with recently restored turkey populations and knew it was necessary to locate gobblers before opening day. That is not to say you can't find good turkey hunters in states where preseason scouting isn't necessary. It's just that those who have learned how to scout often have an edge come opening day.

Scouting has many advantages, but a few stand out above the rest: First, you will know precisely where to begin hunting. You may also learn the habits of the bird you will hunt. Even better, you may get one big step ahead of

Early-season success depends upon preseason scouting. The more you know about the turkey you are after, the better the odds of getting him on opening day.

other hunters. Thanks to the gobbler's big mouth, serious turkey hunters know that hunting pressure is responsible for many unfilled tags every spring. Finally, preseason scouting is one way to avoid the tough late hunting season. Some hunters consistently bag their birds the first few days of the season because they scouted effectively.

Before getting into locating gobblers, you must first find areas with potential. Today, that can be almost any location. We have learned that turkeys favor agricultural areas, small woodlots, bottomlands, and vast areas of timber. In fact, it is difficult to say what type of habitat the wild turkey prefers most. If there is an area that does not yet harbor birds, there is a good chance that it will someday.

Since seeing is believing, a hunter may learn the whereabouts of many gobblers with the aid of their vehicle. That is, providing they can see open fields where turkeys often congregate in flocks in late winter and early spring. However, this tactic can work against you as the hunting season draws near. Several weeks before the spring season debuts, it is common to see large flocks of turkeys. But the flocks break up just before the breeding begins. The gobblers go their separate ways, as do the hens, and could end up a long distance away. Thus, most hunters prefer to spend their scouting time listening for gobbling.

ROOST SITES AND GOBBLING

In a previous chapter, I discussed peak gobbling periods. Peak no. 1 usually occurs at the onset of breeding, or about when the spring hunting season begins in most states. Gobbling begins several weeks before the peak, intensifying daily. I usually begin listening for gobbling two or three weeks before the hunting season, but I am out there every chance I get when the season is only days away.

When you're hoping to hear a turkey gobble, there are good areas and there are areas to avoid. Common sense tells us we should be there before dawn, when the gobblers do most of their talking from the roost. Additionally, you must find a preferred location and spend more time standing than walking. When you're moving, a gobbling bird can be mighty hard to hear even when he's nearby. If you do hear him when you are moving, you will have a difficult time determining his precise whereabouts.

Common sense also tells us to choose a listening area from a high point if possible, and to avoid standing near streams or anything else that will distort our ability to hear a turkey gobble. However, there is a flip side to standing on a high point to listen. If the wind blows, you are probably better off listening along the side of the ridge or from the valley below. When scouting in flatlands, select an area in the open, not in the middle of a canopy of timber. Again, an open area will work against you just as the top of a ridge will work against you when the wind blows.

How far away can you hear a gobble on a still morning from a suitable location? There is no precise answer since every area differs. It also depends on the location of the turkey and the direction he faces when gobbling. I have heard turkeys gobble from one mile away and perhaps farther when conditions were favorable, but I love hearing a bird that is within a few hundred yards. I can usually pinpoint his roost site before he stops gobbling and may learn his habits after he flies down.

The need to locate several turkeys is vital to success. Finding one is good, but two or three is much better. I look at it this way: When hunting public ground, it may be necessary to find several birds because you never know if another hunter has learned the location of the same turkey you've discovered. The same can happen when hunting private land, simply because a gobble can attract a hunter from afar.

Several years ago, I had located a prime candidate for opening morning. With the exception of what he ate for breakfast, I knew everything about this turkey. I also knew that he was mine come opening morning, provided another hunter did not show or a breeding hen interfere. Fifteen minutes before dawn, after the bird gobbled once, another hunter came in behind me, walked past, and flushed the bird

To learn the whereabouts of a gobbler's roost site, arrive early and select a vantage point to listen for gobbling.

in the dark. I headed back to the vehicle and drove to a second location where I had found another customer the previous day. One hour later, I left the woods with a gobbler stuffed in my turkey vest.

Although it is advantageous to locate a gobbler's roost site, it does not necessarily mean he will be there when opening day arrives. While some gobblers will fly up in the same general area every evening, they seldom select a particular roost tree. One time he may be one hundred yards in one direction, the next time he may be four hundred yards the other way. Then there are times when he changes roost areas because he was flushed once too often, was frightened by a predator, or simply moved to find hens. Normally, the larger the area, the better the chance he will roost farther away one day than he did previously.

STRUTTING ZONES AND TRAVEL ROUTES

By learning the movements and habits of the gobbler you locate, you will know where to go when he is on the roost and when he leaves the roost. However, you must avoid getting too close to a roosted turkey, since flushing him might push him to another roost site.

The best way to pattern the gobbler after he flies down from the roost is to sit tight and listen. If he moves away from you, follow him and stay a safe distance. Surprisingly, most gobblers have something in mind when they leave the roost. If a hen does not intercept them, they will usually travel in a consistent direction. This travel route may exist in any type of terrain, but you can bet there is a strutting zone at the other end that interests them.

It helps to know where a gobbler goes when he leaves the roost. Many travel directly to strutting zones, often located in open areas or along old roadbeds.

Strutting zones are nothing more than locations where turkeys spend time listening for sounds of hens and waiting for hens to come to them. They may be the top of a ridge, an open field, or an opening in a cutover area. One thing is certain. A gobbler wants to be noticed by hens and will usually choose an area where he is visible. When he arrives at a strutting zone, he moves back and forth with his feathers beautifully displayed, drumming and spitting.

If you have followed a gobbling bird only to realize that he is staying in one location, there is a good chance the bird has arrived at a strutting zone. His gobbling often subsides minutes after he arrives. This depends on the nature of the individual turkey, of course. However, after locating a strutting zone and determining the direction of travel, the hunter knows precisely where to go if he does not lure the gobbler into range at dawn when the bird first flies down from the roost.

Turkeys have a way of wanting to go in a certain direction. It is much easier to call in a bird if you are ahead of him when he moves. Getting a turkey to turn around and walk in a different direction is like trying to slip daylight past a rooster.

LOCATING SIGN

When you find turkey sign such as tracks, scratchings, feathers, and droppings, you've done half of your scouting. Reading that sign is what spring scouting is really all about.

Turkey tracks, for instance, can tell you a lot more than just the fact that a bird was there. A large track, one that is 4 to 4½ inches long, tells me that a gobbler was in the area, and perhaps for a particular reason. If you find such tracks,

If you find large turkey tracks (four inches or longer), look for wing drag marks that may indicate a strutting zone.

look closely for signs of strutting. A turkey may come to the area to feed, but marks in the leaves or dirt where the turkey's wings dragged on the ground provides proof that he is strutting in the area.

Droppings also indicate the sex of the bird. The droppings of a gobbler are usually one to two inches long and shaped like the letter "J," whereas hen droppings are straighter and often spiraled. Numerous droppings may also indicate a strutting zone or roost site.

Feathers are found throughout turkey range, but numerous feathers in one spot usually indicate a roost site. Of course, turkeys roost in many areas, including pine thickets, the hillsides and valleys of hardwoods, and near water. Determining if gobblers are actually using a roost site is a dif-

You may find feathers anywhere in the turkey's range when scouting. Finding numerous feathers may provide proof of a roost site.

ferent story. Look for fresh droppings and consider returning at dawn to listen for gobbling.

Turkeys scratch daily to find food. The number of scratchings in any area will vary according to the season, terrain, and food availability. Scratchings may provide evidence of turkeys visiting a given woodlot consistently, but they do not tell you the direction the birds are traveling. When you find scratchings, they usually wind around here, there, and sometimes everywhere. Nevertheless, fresh scratchings do indicate that birds are spending time in the area and provide you with a good place to set up in the off-hours of the morning or afternoons when the gobbling subsides. Unfortunately, turkeys may visit the freshly scratched area when you cannot be there. Since it is the turkey's nature to feed after leaving the roost, a freshly scratched area could even indicate a roost site nearby.

ANALYZE YOUR TURF

I cannot overemphasize the need to know your area before the spring hunting begins. You should know every ditch, creek, ridge, and fence line. Gobblers are finicky characters when it comes to walking into a turkey call, and they do not mind heading in the opposite direction when something is in the way.

Once during the late season, I set up on a gobbler during midmorning in unfamiliar territory. He was quite lonely and desperate to find a lady friend. I know that because he closed the gap from three hundred yards to sixty yards only minutes after answering my first call. Once he hit the sixty-yard mark, however, he held his ground. He continued walking back and forth, gobbling with every breath, but he wouldn't come closer. After twenty minutes of attempting to get me to come to him, he simply turned and walked away. Nothing I said could change his mind.

After the ordeal ended, I walked over to where the gobbler had hung up. As it turns out, a fence no more than four feet tall had saved his life. He could easily have walked under or flown over it, but he was obstinate. On the other hand, had I known the area, I could have set up across the fence and killed that turkey in the time it took to put on my face mask and gloves.

There are a couple of ways to learn a hunting area. Perhaps the best way is simply to walk it. This method is slow but effective. It is also a good way to get into shape for opening day. Turkey hunting is strenuous, but I love walking the woods, hoping it will keep me around for another season. My preacher once told the congregation, "I'm not sure if exercise will help you live longer, but at least you will die healthy."

Topographic and aerial maps are essential tools for any hunter. They cannot do all the work for you, but they provide a start. I have a file stuffed full of topo maps that I use annually. You can order individual topo maps from survey offices, or purchase CD-rom disks that include topo maps of a particular state. The folks at DeLorme also publish the *Gazetteer,* which includes topo maps of entire states. Each book costs $19.95. For more information, contact DeLorme, P.O. Box 298, Yarmouth, ME 04096. Aerial maps may be available locally in your area.

You should know the terrain before your hunt begins. First obtain topographic maps of the area, then rely on footwork for the remainder of your scouting.

Hunters always wonder just how far off the roads they should get to avoid other hunters. That is a good question, but there are no guarantees. I once packed three miles into a public hunting site. It was a walk-in-only area, and I assumed there would be no competition. Wrong! I was surrounded by other hunters on opening day and had to pack out immediately.

Getting in deep, regardless of whether you are on public land, is not always the smart thing to do. Sometimes it works, and sometimes it does not. However, never overlook gobblers you locate near roads, particularly busy county roads and highways, since many hunters do overlook such locations.

Calling to turkeys before the spring hunting season begins is taboo. Some hunters do this to build their calling confidence. However, calling to turkeys when scouting is one sure way to create call-shy gobblers and spoil a hunting area. I have heard some hunters say they do this only in areas where they will not hunt. While this may be good for them, it certainly does not help someone else who's hunting that area. If you must use a call to locate a gobbling bird before the season, always use a locator call.

CHAPTER 5
THE AMBUSH
LOCATION

YOUR FIRST SETUP IS CRITICAL TO SUCCESS

When you look for a setup to begin calling, always consider that you may have to shoot from that location. It could be that you will not shoot from that location—you may have to get up and move more times than you ever imagined—in fact, it's rare to kill a turkey from your first ambush location. However, I always consider the first setup vital to my success. I believe the perfect setup is always available regardless of the terrain. You see, any ambush location is perfect if that is where you kill the bird. If you believe this, you will spook fewer turkeys and be better prepared to shoot when a gobbler walks in.

I would wager a dozen of my wife's oatmeal raisin cookies that most turkeys are spooked because a hunter just had

77

to keep looking for a better setup. You know how it goes; you sit in one place for about thirty seconds and see another ambush location that looks even better. As the old saying goes, "The grass is always greener on the other side." Looking for a better setup takes time, however, and time is something we may not have. Several factors determine how much time we have, but it is always best to assume that the right time to sit down and call to a turkey is now.

When selecting an ambush location, consider safety first. The standby rule is to set up against a large tree (preferably wider than your shoulders) so no other hunters will see you if they approach from behind. If they come in from another direction, you can see them. Turkey hunting is not a dangerous sport, but carelessness does occur. It boils down to positively identifying your target before shooting. Humans look nothing like turkeys, but there is always that one individual out there to watch for.

Do I always sit against a large tree? Absolutely not. If I did, I would kill fewer turkeys. Sometimes finding a large tree is impossible. To do that, you might need to move a long distance away from a gobbling turkey or directly toward him. For this reason, I keep safety on my mind but accept the ambush location that will give me the best chance to kill the turkey. I often sit against a little tree, boulder, or logjam, and in some situations against nothing at all.

On one occasion, a turkey gobbled sixty yards away, just over a small hill ahead of me. I dropped immediately and sat on my rear in the middle of some saplings, with no cover around me and no tree against my back. I put on my face mask and gloves, called gently to the turkey, and shouldered my gun. He answered my call and topped the

If you hear a turkey gobble nearby, select an ambush location immediately, even if it is not a preferred setup. The more time you spend looking, the more you risk being detected by a gobbler.

hill seconds later in full strut. The bird never knew what hit him. Had I looked for another setup, I would not have killed that gobbler. I could not have moved forward or to the side without risking the turkey seeing me.

Many times, I have found it necessary to sit in the worst locations imaginable because I knew it was the best and only way to kill the turkey. On other occasions, I have had to remain standing when calling.

Last spring my wife, Vikki, and I were moving along the edge of a field thirty minutes before dawn. We knew the habits of one gobbler and knew that he was tough to set up on. Whenever you called to him, he would answer and walk into the field. However, since he always roosted near the edge of the field, we could not set up in the woodlot that surrounded him. Therefore, I positioned Vikki in a briar thicket a few yards off the field. It was the only decent spot where she could set up. Still, if the gobbler came out as expected, she would have a tough time getting the gun shouldered and only one shooting lane. Twenty minutes after dawn, and after answering a few gentle love yelps, he appeared. He cooperated further by strutting and turning his tail feathers toward her. She promptly took advantage of this stroke of luck and shouldered the gun. A moment later, the shot rang out and the five-year-old turkey toppled.

I have heard that it is better to call a turkey uphill than downhill. I believe in this theory, but I won't go out on a limb to make sure I call a turkey uphill every time. Why would anyone want to spend several minutes and risk getting spotted to circle a turkey that happens to be uphill when you hear him? If the bird is close, I will flop down and call to him. If he's eager to respond, he will probably walk downhill.

If I plan to sit in a given area for a long time, I will often choose an ambush location in fallen timber or thickets. I do this to reduce the possibility of an approaching turkey seeing me. I also know that I get the twitches after sitting for an hour or so. Normally, I do not care for this style of hunting (I love to stay on the move to locate a vocal turkey), but now and again, you must use the sit-tight tactic. I also rely on the seat cushion that is attached to my hunting vest. It keeps my bottom dry and provides comfort and patience.

You do not always need cover around you, but it has advantages when the cautious eyes of a wary gobbler are looking for you. Yes, a turkey coming to a call wants to see something convincing, and he will scan the area cautiously. On the other hand, any dense brush that hides you could also hinder you when it comes time to shoot.

Early in the season, before the foliage has blossomed, you often find yourself hunting in open woods, where it is downright tough to kill turkeys. Some areas are more open than others, but any turkey has a problem coming to something he can hear but not see. A bird is more likely to come in, however, if you choose your setup carefully in the open woods.

The farther a turkey can see when approaching you, the less chance he will walk into range. Thus, it makes sense to set up where your visibility is only about fifty yards. In fact, you will appreciate the turkey being in range, or almost in

Veteran hunters seldom call to a turkey before they have chosen a setup and are ready to kill. A turkey may approach you without making a sound, looking for something to move.

range, when he waltzes into view. If the turkey can see seventy-five yards or more, and there is no hen in plain view, he will not fall victim to your most seductive hen calls. For this reason, it's best to choose a setup where the turkey cannot see a long distance.

In hilly country, try setting up just off the top of a hill if a turkey is on the other side. This forces him to get on top of the hill to see the hen. If you cannot set up near the top of a hill, try an ambush location behind a thicket. If hiding is a problem, consider lying on your belly.

An approaching gobbler usually knows where the hen should be. They have a cunning way of pinpointing a turkey call, even from a considerable distance. Sometimes you can fool the gobbler a little by turning your body away from him and calling toward the opposite direction. This tactic works especially well in open woods.

Many turkey hunters choose their camouflage clothing to blend with their surroundings. However, movement will get you in trouble even if you look precisely like the tree you're sitting against. Turkeys take any moving object that cannot be positively identified as something that wants to eat them. Since you are a predator, you must hunt like other predators. Move only when the turkey's eyes are hidden, by either a tree or his strutting tail feathers, and remember that turkeys never look for answers when a question arises.

A right-handed shooter should avoid facing into an approaching turkey after setting up. Turkeys have a knack of coming in on your right or left side and seldom come straight to you. Many will actually circle and come in behind you. When I set up, I face a little to the right of where I expect the bird to appear. Being a right-handed shooter, I can swing a long way to my left to shoot. A left-handed shooter should face a little to the left so he or she will have room to swing right.

I also consider the surrounding trees after setting up. A few large trees between my ambush location and the fifty-yard mark offer plenty of opportunities for the turkey's head to be hidden, giving me a chance to shoulder my gun unseen. However—and I've said this before—I don't worry about trees when a turkey is gobbling a short distance away. If there are no trees, fallen timber, or thickets to hide the eyes of the approaching turkey, do not be afraid to shoulder your gun before the bird comes into view. This can be physically stressful if you use a heavy shotgun, but it is one sure way of knowing you are prepared.

Many hunters prefer to set up in areas where a turkey will be in range as soon as he is visible. Choose an ambush location where you can see no more than 40 or 50 yards.

The archer often needs to set up differently than the shotgun hunter. Most veteran bowhunters prefer to get behind a large tree or use a camo blind. Drawing the bow is difficult when a turkey is close, and impossible if the turkey's head is not hidden. For this reason, some archers will wait to draw their bow until the turkey passes by.

You may have to choose a setup in a thick area. I don't like setting up where my visibility is limited to twenty or twenty-five yards, but sometimes you have to take what you get. Normally, a turkey prefers not to approach in dense brush and may hang up outside of the area, waiting for you to make a move. (You can read about gobblers that hang up in chapter 8.) But sometimes a gobbler will walk in. I've seen them come into some areas that could hide an ele-

During the early hunting season, open woods are common. A gobbler that can see a long distance will seldom come waltzing in to your calls.

phant. You might consider standing up behind a tree in a thick area. This may give you more visibility than sitting against a tree.

Regardless of where you intend to set up, avoid making any calls until you have positioned yourself perfectly and have everything ready to go. Many hunters call before they have selected an ambush location. This can lead to trouble. If you are fumbling around trying to pick out a spot to sit, or still in the process of getting your face mask and gloves on, you could be spotted by the approaching bird. Always assume that a turkey has an interest in your call. He may or may not gobble back, but he could begin walking to you as soon as you make the first sound.

CHAPTER 6
WORKING SUNRISE GOBBLERS

TACTICS FOR FOOLING A ROOSTED GOBBLER

Spring turkey hunters dearly love the pink light of the morning—the mystical time of day when creatures come alive in the woods. Songbirds, crows, and owls begin serenading the countryside, only to be interrupted by the king himself. And what a wonderful treat it is to hear that familiar "gobble-obble-obble." Whether the heart-pounding sound is near or far, it brings hope and satisfaction to the spring turkey hunter.

Of course, there is no guarantee you will a kill a turkey just because you've heard him gobble. In fact, the work has just begun. You must move to the bird, choose a setup, hope another hunter does not interfere, and apply calling tactics that differ from those you use to work birds that have left the roost.

First you must locate a candidate. Most of us hate hunting days that begin negatively. If we do not hear a turkey gobble in the early morning hours, frustration promptly sets in—followed by panic. Doing our homework and locating gobblers before any hunt day will aid us in hearing turkeys at dawn, but there is never a guarantee. If we do not hear a turkey gobble, the next step is to find a gobbling bird, or to make one gobble.

Choosing a vantage point from which to listen for turkeys in the early morning hours is common sense. Sometimes this makes the difference in hearing or not hearing a gobble. I have often walked a mile or more to make certain

Every turkey hunter wants to hear a gobbling bird at dawn. First give a turkey the chance to gobble on his own. If you don't hear one, then it's time to resort to a locator call in an effort to make him gobble.

Arrive early at a preferred area to listen. High ridges and open areas will increase your chances of hearing a bird gobble.

I would be in the right location before dawn. You must use caution, though, to make certain you do not get too close to a roosted turkey. Getting too close will affect your chance of hearing the bird gobble and may cause him to flush before dawn arrives. However, on one occasion it actually helped me to bump into a bird in the dark hours.

Several years ago, after walking a half mile along a ridge in the dark, I heard the putts of a turkey roosted no more than sixty yards from where I stood. I could see the silhouetted turkey on a limb and had no idea if the alerted bird was a gobbler or hen, but I thought it best to find a place to sit down and not move. With sunrise minutes away, I backed up a few feet and sat down "behind" a large beech tree. I slipped on my face mask and gloves, placed a diaphragm call in my mouth, and waited for the outcome of my misfortune.

To my amazement, the turkey gobbled ten minutes later, after hearing my muffled sneeze. Obviously, as the sky lightened, he had forgotten about me and decided to carry on with the usual morning ritual. I waited a few more minutes and then sent him a string of gentle tree yelps. I did not have time to think about my next move, for I suddenly heard the flapping of wings and then saw him gliding through the air straight at me. The bird hit the leaves about thirty yards to my left and began walking past me. As soon as his head disappeared behind a huge oak, I shouldered the gun. A moment later the turkey lay motionless.

Like many hunters, I have bumped into my share of roosted turkeys. Never have I been so lucky as I was that day, but it does go to show you that many gobblers want to talk at sunrise. Love is in the air, and most gobblers want to say, "Here I am." Many look for any excuse to gobble, including the sound of your favorite locator call.

Although many hunters use locator calls at dawn, I believe it is more advantageous to see if a turkey will gobble on his own. The wisdom of using a hen call before a turkey gobbles is also questionable. This only alerts a turkey to your position before you even know if he exists.

The more ground you cover in the predawn hours, the better, providing you like getting exercise. Moving at prime gobbling time is not recommended, however, since it will interfere with your hearing. I suggest you get to a predetermined point to listen before the gobbling begins and stick around at least twenty minutes or so after daybreak. Some turkeys gobble earlier than others do.

The author bagged this gobbler moments after it flew down from the roost. Amazingly, even though the turkey spotted the hunter and putted in the dark, it forgot all about the intruder and began gobbling at daylight anyway.

This characteristic may vary daily with any bird, due to weather and moods.

If you do not hear a gobble and prime time has passed, use a locator call before moving. You may be surprised to hear a response from a turkey that did not feel like talking earlier. If you do not hear a gobble, move a short distance and try the locator call again. Always start quietly, increasing the volume of the locator call only if you do not get a response.

After hearing a turkey gobble, get as close as possible to his roost tree without spooking him. The ability to judge the distance of a gobble accurately comes with experience. The more turkeys you pursue at dawn, the better you will get at knowing how far away a bird is. Terrain, foliage, wind, and the direction the bird is facing will affect the volume of his gobbles.

They say that closeness counts in horseshoes and ring toss. Well, it also counts in turkey hunting. The closer you can get to a roosted gobbler, the better. The closer you are to him when you begin calling, the less distance he has to travel to get to you. If he has to travel a long distance, the chance increases that something will go wrong before he reaches your position.

Most veteran hunters like to set up about 150 yards from a roosted gobbler, but there is no rule. If you are sure a turkey will not spot you if you move a few yards closer, do not hesitate. Every situation is different, so you must judge each accordingly. It could be that you will need to stay 200 yards away to keep from being spotted if you're hunting in open woods. On the other hand, I have managed to get to within sixty or seventy yards of a roosted bird

Closeness counts when setting up on a roosted gobbler. The less distance he has to travel to get to you, the better the chance that nothing will go wrong before he gets to you.   (Credit: Vikki Trout)

when I knew he could not see me. You can't usually get that close, but if you do, the bird may fly down and land within shooting range.

Wake-up time is dawn, so I don't recommend calling to a turkey before then (you must also think about regulations in the area that you hunt). But the earlier you call to a turkey, the sooner he may get to you. Yes, some eager birds will fly down to meet a hen in the dark, but that is uncommon.

When you begin calling to a roosted gobbler, do so quietly. Hens do not holler "YELP, YELP, YELP, YELP" when they begin to stir in the morning. Instead, they prefer tree calls, such as "yelp, yelp, yelp, yelp." Always begin with gentle

Hens are quite vocal early in the morning at wake-up time. However, their vocalization is usually limited to gentle tree yelps, clucks, and sometimes fly-down cackles.

calls and increase the tempo only after a turkey is on the ground—that is, providing you need to call again.

Some hunters say that a turkey always hears your gentle tree yelps and knows exactly where you are. That theory can be argued. Turkeys have a good sense of hearing, but I have hunted with some guys who yelped so softly that I could barely hear them ten yards away. Make certain you use enough volume to be heard.

If a gobbler does not respond to your tree yelps immediately, do not assume he did not hear your calls. Some gobblers answer, and some do not. Some hunters have a tendency to pick up the calling tempo if a gobbler does not answer, but the fact is that the turkey may have an interest even though he doesn't respond. Some will gobble thirty seconds after you call. Others might not answer at all but can hardly wait to meet with you nevertheless. Several gobblers have come in to my calls right after flying down from the roost, despite the fact that they never answered one from the roost.

You might consider combining gentle clucks with tree yelps when working a roosted gobbler. Another effective call is the cackle. Hens often cackle when they fly down from the roost. Many times the cackle will entice a gobbler to leave the roost, particularly if you use a mouth diaphragm and imitate flapping wings. By rapidly pounding the palm of your hand against your thigh or buttocks, you can make a sound similar to a turkey's wings flapping. One hunter I know uses a cutoff pair of blue jeans. He trims the jeans just above the knee. This leaves a portion of each leg on the jeans as a handle for him to grab. To imitate flapping wings, he holds a leg of the jeans in each hand with the pants upside down and yanks the legs back and forth rapidly.

Primos Hunting Calls manufactures the Real Wing, real turkey wing feathers connected to a handle that you can bang against your body or flap in the air to simulate a flying turkey. You can also use the Real Wing to simulate turkeys fighting and scratching.

Scotch Game Calls, a division of Pete Rickard, Inc., produces the Scotch Double Wing Call, a two-piece camouflage material with two plastic dowels. You can easily create the sound of wings flapping by holding the ends of the Double Wing and bringing both hands together and apart one or two times.

A tom turkey often gobbles after he flies down from the roost. In fact, an experienced hunter can listen to a gobble and determine when a bird is on the ground, as the sound is more muffled than when he gobbles from the roost. This is helpful since you can change to another calling strategy, or get up and move to another location if necessary.

Since hens could be nearby, always listen for the sounds of other turkeys when you begin calling to a roosted gobbler. Hearing their soft tree yelps will let you know that you have another situation on your hands. You may need to move closer to the gobbler, or get between the gobbler and hens if possible.

When a tom turkey begins gobbling, he is attempting to attract hens. He loves to see them on the ground and fly down to them, so it is understandable that a hen or two in the area can spoil your hunt. They can move to him while you cannot. However, if you get close to the roosted gobbler, your hen talk may entice him to get to you before the hens get to him. He will probably think you're just another one of the hens in the area. Chapter 10 discusses methods to beat gobblers with hens.

You must be patient when working a roosted gobbler. When turkeys are on the ground, you can call too little or too much; the personality of the turkey you are working determines how much calling you should do. However, when you set up and call to a gobbler on the roost, you should call very little. The more you call to him, the longer he may stay in his roost tree. Beginning hunters often make this mistake. When I started turkey hunting, I always called and called and called. I remember one gobbler that sat in the tree for three hours. He gobbled the entire morning but never flew down

Aggressive calling tactics may keep a gobbler in the tree longer, strutting and drumming, waiting on the hen to come to him.

until I moved too close and he spotted me. I soon learned why aggressive calling at dawn seldom works.

Hunters often wonder if they should go to the first turkey they hear, even if he is a long way off. Many veteran hunters say yes, arguing that you may not hear another turkey closer. I cannot give a definite answer to that question since stipulations exist. For instance, if you have been hearing a turkey in a given area for several days, it may pay to sit tight and wait for him to talk. The idea of going to the first bird you hear is based on making certain that you will have a turkey to work in the early morning hours before the gobbling activity decreases. I look at it this way: If turkeys are not gobbling once they hit the ground, I am probably not going to take off after one a mile away since he will probably be on the ground and tight-mouthed before I get there. You must also consider that a turkey may gobble closer to you if you wait.

On several occasions, I have chased a gobbling turkey from one ridge to the next. You know how it goes. You hear one five hundreds yards away on the next ridge. So you take off and arrive sweated up and worn out a short time later. You wait but do not hear the turkey you came after, but you do hear one gobbling his fool head off on the ridge you just came from. The fact is, you can hear some turkeys gobble from a distance more easily than if they are close. One little hill between you and a bird can muffle his gobbles, while a bird on a distant ridge comes through loud and clear because nothing separates you and him except air.

Despite what many hunters believe, roost departure time is not necessarily the best time to kill a turkey. I say this because many hunters panic if they do not get on a gobbling turkey early in the morning. Some of the best opportunities arrive after the birds are on the ground, during the second and even the third hour following dawn.

A few years ago, I did a magazine article on the times of day when many spring turkeys were harvested. Surprisingly, in the three states that I researched for the article, hunters killed more birds after the first hour of the morning than before. Many factors probably contributed to the statistics showing the time of kill, but you can bet that fewer turkeys are killed during the first hour because they have plenty of things to do after leaving the roost, such as getting grit, feeding and sometimes moving to a certain area. Responding to a hen call may be secondary to many gobblers until they have taken care of other business and waited a short while for a hen to come to them.

BEST HUNTING TIMES

The first hour of daylight is not necessarily the best time to kill a turkey. The tables indicate harvest times, quantity harvested and percentage of total harvest as reported by three states.

INDIANA

Morning Times	Total Birds Harvested	Percentage of Total Harvest
1st hour 5 a.m. to 6 a.m.	97	2.8
2nd hour 6 a.m. to 7 a.m.	1267	36.5
3rd hour 7 a.m. to 8 a.m.	820	23.6
4th hour 8 a.m. to 9 a.m.	484	13.9
5th hour 9 a.m. to 10 a.m.	362	10.4
6th hour 10 a.m. to 11 a.m.	261	7.5
7th hour 11 a.m. to 12 p.m.	171	4.9

SOUTH CAROLINA

Morning Times	Total Birds Harvested	Percentage of Total Harvest
1st hour 5 a.m. to 6 a.m.	12	0.5
2nd hour 6 a.m. to 7 a.m.	167	6.3
3rd hour 7 a.m. to 8 a.m.	917	34.9
4th hour 8 a.m. to 9 a.m.	747	28.4
5th hour 9 a.m. to 10 a.m.	362	13.7
6th hour 10 a.m. to 11 a.m.	190	7.2
7th hour 11 a.m. to 12 p.m.	130	4.9

WISCONSIN

Morning Times	Total Birds Harvested	Percentage of Total Harvest
1st hour 5 a.m. to 6 a.m.	76	5.1
2nd hour 6 a.m. to 7 a.m.	424	28.7
3rd hour 7 a.m. to 8 a.m.	360	24.4
4th hour 8 a.m. to 9 a.m.	243	16.5
5th hour 9 a.m. to 10 a.m.	154	10.4
6th hour 10 a.m. to 11 a.m.	126	8.5
7th hour 11 a.m. to 12 p.m.	94	6.4

CHAPTER 7
BOSS BIRDS VS.
BACHELOR GROUPS

WORKING A GROUP OF GOBBLERS DIFFERS FROM WORKING ONE DOMINANT GOBBLER

There I was, lying flat on my belly in mud with a few briars doing their best to drain me of vital body fluids. Nonetheless, it would be worth the effort if I remained invisible to the four eyes that were scanning the woods for a hen. I had called to the bachelor group moments earlier, then gotten up to move to a better ambush location. After spotting one of the turkeys, I had dropped to the ground immediately. I dared not move.

The two gobblers passed by me at twelve paces, their beards swaying back and forth. A minute later, they disappeared over a rise and went on their merry way. With the two boys now out of view and my composure regained, I crawled down to a small dogwood tree and began calling. I felt lucky that the birds hadn't seen me and certain that they would come back.

Unlike the typical boss bird (the independent rascal who loves to breed all the hens and make hunters look like fools), a group of gobblers is often easy to call into range. In fact, these two turkeys responded not once, but twice. The first time I called, both birds gobbled and headed straight for me. That was when I moved and was almost spotted. After I reached the dogwood tree and sent a string of love yelps over the hill, both birds gobbled back. Then they gobbled again, closer than before. Then I saw them walking over the hill, strutting in all their glory. Not one to wait for something to go wrong, I took advantage of the first one to walk into shotgun range.

Bachelor groups, consisting of two or more gobblers, are often easier to call up than an individual boss gobbler.

Not all bachelor groups respond quite so readily as those two did, but most come easier than the gobbler that travels alone, particularly the mature boss birds that do most of the breeding. Who knows which you will deal with the next time you set up and call to a turkey, but you should be aware that tactics differ.

Bachelor groups usually consist of two or three gobblers, sometimes more. Although large gobbler flocks, common in the winter months, have usually broken up by the time the spring season begins, two or more gobblers may travel and roost together even during the mating season. Many are two year olds, but sometimes a bachelor group will include an older gobbler. These turkeys are buddies and will often gobble simultaneously when answering hen calls and locator calls. This is the best way to determine if you are dealing with a bachelor group. When the first turkey gobbles, another gobbler or two usually interrupts his delivery. This is not always the case, however; sometimes you will be fooled when only one bird gobbles but two or more turkeys come walking in.

A boss bird, the turkey that travels alone, is usually identifiable because you hear only his gobble. However, not every gobbler that travels alone is a boss bird. On the contrary, some two-year-old gobblers choose not to join bachelor groups.

Knowing that you are dealing with a mature gobbler, one three years old or older, is never easy to determine for certain. While a mature white-tailed buck can be identified by his large headgear, a turkey's spurs are almost impossible to see. Nor do I believe that you can tell his age by the sound of his gobble. Some hunters claim that a boss gobbler has more of a deep, thunderous gobble than that of a two year old, but that theory has yet to be proved. Personally, I have heard two-year-old birds sound like the most ferocious beasts in the woods.

I can better determine if I am dealing with a mature boss bird by his actions. For instance, gobblers that do most of the breeding gobble less frequently than two-year-old birds as the morning progresses. This is because the hens respond to the mature gobbler—of course, that can change as the season progresses and more hens begin nesting. Nevertheless, often every two-year-old gobbler in a bachelor group will respond to every call. Additionally, boss gobblers seldom advance as quickly to your calls. They are older and a whole lot more cautious than the gobbler that is not yet breeding hens.

Finding and killing a boss gobbler is a tough challenge. Just look at the statistics in the area you hunt. No matter where that is, two-year-old turkeys make up the bulk of the harvest every year. Hatches and survival rates have some bearing on this, but you can bet that many mature gobblers survive because they do not fall for the same hunting tactics that fool younger gobblers.

Although most of us would love to kill a boss gobbler, we will usually take a two-year-old bird when the opportunity arises. It is also true that most of us do not head for the woods in pursuit of a mature trophy gobbler. Now and again we may become obsessed with killing a gobbler that has outsmarted us day after day, and that we assume is a boss gobbler, but most often we're happy when a bachelor group with swinging beards shows up.

I love bumping heads with a bachelor group, because the birds seem to love taking chances. I am unsure if it is

Because mature gobblers do most of the breeding, they are often more difficult to call up than two-year-old birds. They may gobble frequently to your calls but are reluctant to move because they fully expect the hens to come to them.

Two-year-old gobblers make up the highest percentage of harvests. However, three-year-old and older birds are often more vulnerable to calls during the late season after the hens begin nesting.

competition (one wanting to get to the hen ahead of another), or if they simply feel brave when traveling with other turkeys. Perhaps the old saying "Safety in numbers" contributes to their overanxious desire to come to turkey calls.

Since bachelor groups seem to respond more readily to turkey calls than boss birds traveling alone, it is often better to be aggressive when you work them. The more you make them gobble, the more anxious they are to get to you. I prefer loud yelps and excited cutts when calling to a group of gobblers. I may also call repeatedly. When they gobble to my first call, I promptly come back with another. This may continue right up to the time the birds come into view.

Bachelor groups also respond to other gobblers. For this reason, you might consider using a gobble tube if you run into a group of gobblers that does not move toward you. *Gobbling* to turkeys is dangerous since it could attract another hunter, but it often works. I believe some bachelor groups feel brave and eager to check out another gobbling turkey. They might have second thoughts if they encounter a tough, mature gobbler, but that won't happen if you are sitting there waiting to smack one in the head with a load of shotgun pellets.

One problem with hunting a boss gobbler is simply being aware that that's what he is. You can't rely on the size of tracks, or the body size of a gobbler that you spot before the hunting season. Some two-year-old turkeys have big feet. And a mature gobbler may lose weight during the breeding season, making him lighter than a younger bird that is not breeding.

I took a three-year-old gobbler one year before writing this book. He weighed 24½ pounds, carried 1⅛-inch spurs, and had a 10-inch beard. No doubt he could be considered a mature gobbler; however, he was not the boss bird of the area. Near the same woods but in an agricultural field that had become a strutting zone, Vikki killed a 22½-pound gobbler with spurs just over 1¼ inches long and a beard that was 11¼ inches long. We knew her turkey did most of the breeding and was probably a four- or five-year-old gobbler even though it weighed considerably less than the bird I harvested.

You may be able to determine that a turkey in your area is a mature boss gobbler by studying his habits. Mature gobblers often travel to strutting zones daily. Such was the case with the gobbler my wife shot. This turkey traveled to

This five-year-old gobbler carried long spurs and a long, thick beard. The author's wife, Vikki, took this bird after she set up near his strutting zone—a small hill in a soybean field only a short distance from the turkey's roost site.

a small open field every morning. Boss gobblers travel to strutting zones fully expecting that the hens will come too.

Late one morning on another occasion, my son, John, encountered a bird that had gobbled in the same vicinity for several days. The turkey always seemed to start gobbling in this area about two hours after dawn. John moved in and set up about one hundred yards from the turkey, but as expected, his calls failed to attract the bird. Since this was his last day to hunt, he decided to take a risk and move closer. He topped a hill and spotted a field that he assumed was the gobbler's strutting zone. When he was within shooting distance of the field, John dropped to the ground and started calling aggressively. The turkey appeared almost as quickly as it responded to the call, only to take a slap on the head with a load of No. 4s. This boss bird carried 1¼-inch spurs.

My experience with mature gobblers has taught me this: If you want to be successful, you have to get close to their strutting zones. Boss birds seldom venture far from those areas, and who can blame them? They get used to visiting a strutting zone every day. They also know that that is where they have the best chance of attracting a breeding hen once the early morning breeding encounters subside.

When calling to a boss gobbler, you might need to try gentle calls, since aggressive ones will sometimes turn off the switch. In the case of the mature turkey that my son took, the bird responded to rapid, loud cutts, probably because the calls were extremely close. Most mature gobblers refuse to move a long distance to get to a hunter making aggressive calls. As dominant turkeys, they have heard it all before, and they may even turn and walk the other away when they hear too much calling. I usually call more sparingly when facing a lonesome turkey, but I monitor his response. If he answers every call and appears to want more, I may get aggressive and call louder. Or I may call more often if that seems to get him to move toward me.

Boss gobblers may also respond to offbeat calling tactics, such as the sounds of fighting hens. This calling tactic often works when other calls fail. Fighting calls may also work on hung-up and call-shy turkeys, which you will read about in the following chapter.

Strategy is probably the best tool to use when bumping heads with a boss. You have to do everything you might not do otherwise. Changing setups repeatedly, scratching the leaves, and even playing the quiet game are often necessary to get a mature turkey to move closer.

The author's son, John Trout III, took this boss gobbler during the late turkey season near the bird's strutting zone. His success was probably due to getting close to the strutting zone and fewer hens being bred.

Your best chance of encountering a boss gobbler may be during the late season. Most of the hens are breeding by then, and the mature turkeys are feeling lonely. Still, you will need to apply your best efforts if you hope to kill a lonesome boss gobbler. Such a grand bird demands—and deserves—nothing less.

CHAPTER 8
HUNG UP OR
CALL SHY?

YOU SHOULD KNOW WHICH TURKEY
YOU ARE DEALING WITH

I seriously doubt that you will face a tougher gobbler than
one that is stubborn and refuses to move. Two turkeys possess this trait in the spring woods: the call-shy gobbler and
the gobbler that hangs up. They are similar in that they
refuse to move closer to the caller. The worst news about
these comparable, yet unique gobblers is that you will usually face such a bird at some point during the hunting season.

These two birds are always tough to kill, but they make
mistakes just like any other gobbler. The first step to killing
an uncooperative gobbler rests in knowing which of the two
birds you are dealing with. Has he refused to respond be-

cause he is call shy, or is it because he has hung up? Knowing the difference can mean tagging or not tagging a bird.

PERSONALITY DIFFERENCES

Both the call-shy turkey and the bird that hangs up may or may not gobble to your calls. Both are capable of answering a call all the time or only some of the time. For this reason, you can't determine which bird you are facing by the way he gobbles. I believe that a call-shy bird does not gobble to calls as often as a bird that hangs up, but nothing about that belief is carved in stone. There are a few differences worth noting, however.

The gobbler that hangs up simply refuses to move. He can advance part of the way to you, or he may simply hold his ground. He usually does not move farther away. The one thing he does, though, is live by the book of nature. It is nature's law that the hens go to him. The gobbler that hangs up is simply sticking to the rules. He may answer every call, begging you to come closer, or he may move closer to you but hold up out of range.

The hung-up gobbler seems to have a knack for knowing the range of your trusty shotgun. He may come forward but stop in his tracks at the fifty- or sixty-yard mark. It is as though there is a danger line that he can see quite well. When this occurs, the hunter is almost helpless. The magic word in that sentence, however, is *almost*. In just a moment, I will get into a few tricks you can use to entice him to come just a little closer.

I believe that hunters assume a turkey to be call shy all too often. The fact is, there are fewer call-shy gobblers running

There are many differences between the gobbler that hangs up out of range and the call-shy turkey. The first step in tagging one is to know which you are dealing with.

in the woods than there are turkeys that hang up. However, when a gobbler doesn't come in to calls, a hunter usually assumes he has been worked before and is therefore call shy.

The call-shy gobbler may be call shy for one or for many reasons. For instance, seeing one too many hunters after coming to a call, hearing too many calls, shyness, and fear of the unknown may affect his willingness to come in to a call or even answer one.

Call-shy birds are similar to gobblers that do not answer calls. Gobblers that do not answer calls are often only "pressured turkeys," which I will discuss in chapter 9, "Public-Land Gobblers." Call-shy turkeys may gobble to your calls more often than pressured turkeys, but they have a problem that is best described as cowardliness. Ultimately, they are downright scared to go over there to investigate what's making that yelping.

HUNG-UP GOBBLER TACTICS

When a gobbler comes toward you but hangs up just out of gun range, you can assume your calling was effective. He stops because he expects you to walk in the rest of the way. After all, he figures he gave a little and so should you.

In such a situation, most of us continue calling, hoping to convince him to come just a little closer. If the bird is headstrong (I've never met a hung-up gobbler that wasn't) that technique won't work. It will take something more convincing to make him move across the imaginary line that separates life from death.

Though we have all heard of scratching the leaves with our hands, few rely on this technique to make a gobbler

When a gobbler hangs up, it seems his sixth sense tells him just how close he should come to your calls. Once he stops and refuses to move, he waits on the hen to come to him.

move. But let me tell you, this tactic does work on hung-up gobblers. I usually include a few subtle calls, such as purrs and clucks, with the scratching. A mouth diaphragm is best for this, since it allows you to call and scratch the leaves simultaneously. If you use only a friction call, scratch the leaves and come right back with the gentle calls. This lets a gobbler know that all is well, but you are somewhat busy trying to stuff your gullet right now. Surprisingly, he may come a few yards closer to have a look.

If a gobbler stops at a considerable distance, say one to two hundred yards away, you may not be facing a hung-up turkey. It could be that the gobbler has hens with him, which means you need to apply different tactics. Most gobblers that hang up are alone and do so less than one hundred yards from your ambush location.

A turkey may also hang up because the area is too open or too thick. If that is the case, you will need to choose a better setup. I discussed choosing setups in open areas previously. This is a good time to mention it again. A turkey will rarely come to a call when he can see for a long distance. If he does not see the hen, he closes the book on that love story. If you set up in a thicket, the bird may get as close as possible but refuse to pass through an area where a predator could reach out and grab him or sneak up on him. However, before you move out of a thicket to select a better ambush location, give the turkey time to show up. I have seen gobblers come into areas where the devil himself wouldn't go.

I have also played the quiet game on hung-up gobblers. When they get close and refuse to move, I stop calling. This often works when other tactics fail. The idea is to make the

If a gobbler hangs up, it could be that your setup is all wrong. If the area is too open or too thick, a gobbler may refuse to move. Try setting up in a different location and calling again.

gobbler sweat and wonder if the hen has left. Sometimes *you* end up sweating, but other times the hung-up gobbler just has to sneak in closer to see what is going on.

You might also consider turning your body away and calling gently. This may make the gobbler think you are leaving, or are farther away than he thought. If you use a mouth diaphragm, just call while facing away from the gobbler. If you use a friction call, you can try keeping the call against your body to muffle the sound, but you will still need to turn around and keep your body between your call and the turkey.

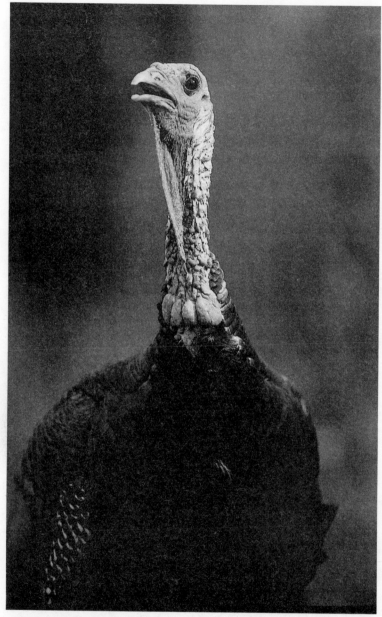

Call-shy gobblers are fearful. Hearing the sweet talk of a hen is seldom enough to boost their confidence.

CALL-SHY GOBBLER TACTICS

When you face a call-shy gobbler, you must understand that he is fearful of something—so fearful that he may or may not answer your calls. He may even go away from you. Sounds like a tough bird to kill, right? Yes, he can be hard to get. However, keep in mind that a wild turkey, even one that is call shy, is quite stupid. Survival instincts make him look sharp, but he lacks the ability to think and reason. That is why some tactics come in handy when working a call-shy gobbler. You can apply a few sneaky methods so that he suddenly discovers something that builds his confidence and takes away his fear.

One tactic that I always rely on when working a call-shy turkey is to change setups repeatedly. Turkey hunters often sit and call and call and call from the same location. When hens talk, they move around a lot. That is precisely what the hunter must do when working a call-shy gobbler. Call to him from one location, then move a short distance and call again. Even a move of twenty or thirty yards is acceptable. He knows where the call is coming from. Sometimes it takes four or five moves to convince him you are the real thing.

You should avoid calling from locations such as old roadbeds or jeep trails. In fact, that is how and where some call-shy turkeys are educated. They did not hatch as call-shy turkeys. That shyness is an activated survival instinct, compliments of us turkey hunters. Every time they gobble, someone closes in and hollers "YELP, YELP, YELP!" Many times the yelping they hear comes from places that hunters walk consistently.

One way to build the confidence of a call-shy gobbler is to change setups sev-eral times. Even a move of 20 or 30 yards can make him believe that all is well.

Although aggressive calling works on some turkeys, it is usually not advisable when working a call-shy gobbler; it may turn the bird away. Gentle talk is best. Call very little and keep the volume low. Yelps, clucks, and purrs are acceptable, but sometimes only purrs and clucks are better.

Once while hunting in Missouri, I moved in to work a call-shy gobbler at dawn, while the bird was on the roost. I knew he was call shy because he had demonstrated that trait when I worked him the previous week. A few other hunters had also worked this particular turkey. I learned that he did not like too much calling. In fact, even one call was pushing it to the max. I waited on the turkey to gobble from the roost and came back with one cluck. He did not answer until about thirty seconds later, as if he were considering the scenario. I applied enough volume to yet another cluck to be heard; then I sat, hoping that would be enough to convince him to come my way at fly-down time.

Fifteen minutes later, the turkey gobbled from the ground. I fought temptation and did not call. Sure enough, he never said another word either. But he did come walking in thirty minutes after he left the roost. His white head and beady little eyes scanned the woods, looking for the hen that made the one cluck. At forty yards he stopped and refused to move, so I accepted the distance between us as reasonable and squeezed the trigger. If the truth be known, other hunters in the area were probably grateful that I removed this troublesome character. This was the kind of bird that can waste away your season.

You might also consider using a different call, such as a gobble, or the sound of fighting hens. Call-shy turkeys are most fearful when they hear common yelps but may not hesitate to respond to something different. Use caution when gobbling, however, because it could attract another hunter to your ambush location.

I have used fighting calls on several occasions to lure call-shy turkeys into range, but one incident stands out in my mind. Several years ago my son, John, and I set up on a turkey in the same area where I had killed a bird a couple of days earlier. The gobbler I killed was with another turkey, which is the bird we had to face.

Naturally, the turkey was a bit call shy, after seeing his buddy knocked to the ground and then watching me come running over to get him. Nonetheless, it was the only bird we had to work that day.

We set up, and John called to the turkey. The gobbler responded only now and then and moved away. We changed

Call-shy turkeys seldom respond to aggressive calling. One exception is the sounds of fighting hens.

locations several times during the next two hours but could-
n't build the bird's confidence. The call-shy turkey would
not come in, and we were running out of options. So I
scooted back behind my son and went to work with fighting
calls. I can still remember the turkey gobbling five times after hearing the sound of the simulated fighting hens. Then
all was quiet. A short time later, John's gun roared. Later,
John related that the two-year-old gobbler came to within
forty-five yards (about the maximum distance at which he
could shoot effectively) and stopped. The fighting hen calls
had come through again.

DECOYING

Decoying can be very effective when you're working a
hung-up or call-shy turkey. Having something there that
looks like the real thing is no guarantee, but using the right
decoy when opportunity allows may increase the chance it
will work. I prefer a hen decoy when facing a call-shy or
hung-up turkey. The rest of the time, gobbler decoys are
probably better than hen decoys, particularly when you face
a gobbler with hens. Nevertheless, the two turkeys we are
discussing will probably want to see Ms. Love herself.
When a bird hangs up just beyond shooting range and sees
the decoy, it is possible he will hold his ground and gobble
for the decoy to come to him. A call-shy turkey may be
quicker to respond than a hung-up gobbler if he sees the
right decoy, but either can look quite stupid on the right day.

I prefer not to use decoys most of the time because they
hinder me. I believe it better to use other strategies, such as
changing setups as needed and using certain calls. Since a

Despite what some hunters believe, you can kill a turkey that is call shy or hangs up when using the right tactics.

decoy takes time to set up, it can slow you down and cause you to be spotted. You are also limited to areas where you can set them up. And since careless hunters shoot a few other hunters every year, you should not take chances and place them in wooded areas where another hunter could get close without your knowing.

The possibility that you will face a turkey that either hangs up or is call-shy on your next hunt is quite good. I fully expect to encounter them every spring. So far, my nightmares have come true. So what are the odds of you scoring on one of these turkeys? I'm sure it isn't very good, but I would rather work a call-shy or hung-up gobbler than no turkey at all.

CHAPTER 9
PUBLIC-LAND
GOBBLERS

HOW TO SCORE IN PRESSURED AREAS

Those who consistently pursue spring gobblers on public lands probably envy those who hunt private lands, and rightfully so. I don't believe anyone would dispute the fact that it is more difficult to kill a turkey on public land. It may be true that some private lands receive extensive hunting pressure, but hunters bombard nearly every public area on opening day.

I live in Indiana and each spring hunt part of Hoosier National Forest. I also travel south to hunt the vast Land Between the Lakes in Kentucky and Tennessee, and west to hunt the Mark Twain National Forest in Missouri. I have hunted other public lands that are not so busy, but these areas have provided me with plenty of frustration and success over the years. I hunt private lands, too. No turkey comes easy, but the public-land gobblers I face are usually much more difficult to call in to range than those I hunt on private lands.

Hunting pressure is responsible for making turkeys tough to kill, and that goes for public and private lands. For instance, about ten to twelve years ago wild turkey restoration was going strong in areas not far from my home. When the county opened to hunting, I jumped at the chance to be there. I ran into many turkeys with suicidal attitudes. None were shy, and nearly every bird I worked came to the call with little or no hesitation. However, hunting pressure has now changed the personalities of the birds. Today, most of these residential gobblers are as difficult to hunt as any public-land turkey.

OPENING-DAY OPPORTUNITIES

One of the best times to enjoy success on public lands is opening day, before the birds take a beating. However, that is easier said than done, since many other hunters have the same idea. Your best chance of filling a tag lies in your ability to know each gobbler, his terrain and his habits, and then jump on him before he has a chance of reacting negatively to hunting pressure. That is good advice for hunting anywhere, but twice as important when hunting on public land.

Scouting to hear gobbling is essential. Pick a turkey and make it a point to go after him at daylight on opening day. Of course, since several other guys might be going after the same turkey, it makes sense to choose your bird wisely. Is it better to find a bird that is located deep in the area? Or are you better off out by a road, assuming others will penetrate the area? I call the shots according to the land I hunt. Public lands with walk-in areas often invite people to get in deep, simply because it's easy to do. If a walk-in area is not offered, most hunters will not penetrate deep because there isn't an easy route to follow. It is sometimes better to find a bird close to a major road if most hunters penetrate the area. If you have several hunters driving roads trying to locate birds, then roads may not be the answer. Consider finding a bird that roosts out of the way. Perhaps you will have to cross a swamp to get to him. Some hunters won't do that. Perhaps the turkey roosts in a valley, making his gobbling hard to hear. I love finding turkeys that are not easily heard.

Once you have located a bird for opening morning, I suggest you learn the terrain and the turkey's habits. Be aware of obstacles that may prevent him from getting to you, such as fence lines or water. You should know where the bird goes after he leaves the roost so you can set up in his line of travel. A two-year-old public-land bird may go out of his way to get to you on opening day, but older gobblers probably won't. And who knows how old the bird is that you face? Never make it hard for a public-land turkey to get to you.

Topographic maps are helpful and can allow you to find access to areas you may not have known existed. Forestry maps may also show you private and public-land boundaries and ways to get close to out-of-the-way sectors of public land.

OUTSMARTING OTHER HUNTERS

Turkeys on public lands get used to hearing calling from places such as logging roads, trails, and county roads. Whenever you set up, do so away from those locations. You

Most public-land turkeys are skeptical about responding to hen talk that comes from logging roads and trails. When setting up to call, choose a place away from such areas.

will be surprised how often a turkey responds to calls when you are set up away from the places people consistently walk. The morning hunt of some people consists of walking a logging road and calling every hundred yards. It might work in some areas but rarely in public areas.

Some hunters aren't patient after making a call. They assume that if a turkey does not gobble, he is not coming. Be aware that public-land birds love to sneak in without saying a word. I can't tell you how many pressured turkeys I have heard putt just when I got up from an ambush location.

While hunting the Mark Twain National Forest one day a few years ago, I had worked a bird for about thirty minutes. The turkey had gobbled a few times but had not responded to my calls positively. The gobbler finally shut down totally, and I sat back and nearly fell asleep, assuming he would never show. An hour later, crushing leaves to my left aroused me. Then I saw him. I flinched, and he saw me. He took off running and was out of sight before I could shoulder the gun. The moral to the story is simple: Gobblers on public lands take their time about coming in and are sneaky about it when they do.

Since most hunters are attracted to numerous turkeys gobbling, it is usually better for you to go after just one. You know how it works; a hunter hears four turkeys gobbling along a certain ridge and can't wait to get there. But that one bird off to himself on another ridge will offer you the best opportunity to work a bird without others interfering. I would prefer to have one turkey in the woods to myself than have ten turkeys and ten hunters.

Interference is a common problem, but I suggest you do not give up just because someone spooked a turkey that you

If another hunter interferes and spooks a gobbler that you are working, stick around. Many gobblers will move only a short distance away and begin gobbling again an hour later.

were working. After the other hunter leaves, sit back and wait. You will be surprised how many spooked turkeys begin gobbling thirty minutes to an hour after a hunter bumps them.

CALLING TACTICS

Since pressured turkeys hear more yelping than any other call, consider trying clucks and purrs. Once an area has been hunted for a day or more, a gobbler may ignore a hunter's yelps. If you get a few hunters calling to turkeys before the season, the birds might even ignore yelping before opening day. However, they do hear other turkey talk from the real thing, particularly common clucks and purrs.

There is a time and place for consistent calling and increased volume. A public area is probably at the bottom of the list. The only time I get aggressive is when I have to compete with hens—but that is another story that you will read about later in this book. Usually, I yelp very little (sometimes not at all); I call gently and only as often as necessary.

If you get a bird gobbling fiercely, it becomes tempting to call more. However, that may not be smart. On public lands, everyone knows that making a bird gobble and gobble usually attracts more hunters. I judge that scenario cautiously. If I must call more to lure the gobbler in, I will not hesitate to do so, providing I have not run into other hunters. If there are several hunters in the area, I will probably call less and hope the bird shows up.

Aggressive calling may not work on pressured birds. Try calling less, with low-volume calls.

BEST DAYS TO HUNT

Although opening day can offer rewards, don't be afraid to hunt the midmorning hours, weekdays, and during the late season. We never know how many hunters are in a public area during these times, but you can bet your luckiest turkey feather that opening day will be crowded, especially if it's on a weekend.

The major factor governing success on public lands is hunting pressure. It affects the personality of the gobbler as well as the hunter. You can't do much about the gobbler's personality, but you can remain positive. Pressured gobblers do make mistakes, and they can be killed. You can also consider hunting at the most opportune times.

Some people give up two hours after daylight because they ran into six other hunters an hour earlier and stopped hearing turkeys ten minutes after dawn. However, it is common for other hunters to evacuate the area and for gobblers to start talking during the midmorning hours. Hunters do kill turkeys every year on public lands between the hours of 10 A.M. and 12 P.M. Consider that hens might be nesting, which leaves more gobblers alone and prone to talk. Even better, a few of those lonesome fellows may just be strutting around waiting to hear anything that sounds like a turkey. If the hens are inactive and other hunters have left, you are the one who can oblige them.

Public lands are usually busiest on the first weekend of the season. However, many hunters give up after the first few days of the season. If your time allows you to hunt on weekdays, or even weekends during the last week of the hunting season, you should do it. I also suggest you go into areas where the hunting pressure was once heavy. There are probably fewer gobblers, and the survivors may talk less, but you can bet there are always some in the area that are hoping to locate a hen.

Another factor to consider is the increasing foliage. During the last few days of the turkey season, the woods are much greener than they were during the first few days. This is to your advantage, since any bird you work will need to come closer to you to see the hen.

Five years ago, I shot a bird late in the first week of the season on heavily hunted public land. With two weeks to go, I began scouting the area in hopes of returning to assist other hunters. I found a couple of birds and returned with my wife during the last week of the season. The first morn-

The late season is sometimes the best time to fill a tag. The author took this gobbler on public land only days before the season ended.

(Credit: Vikki Trout)

ing she took a respectable two-year-old bird. Two days later, I came back with a friend. The first day was tough, but the second day he filled his tag. My son came in on the last day and took his bird. From my experience, that year was better than most at that particular public area, but it does go to show you that good things can happen after other hunters quit.

It's not that the birds get easier (sometimes they do) during the late season; it's just that you can work them without interference. Such was the case with each of the birds I just mentioned. Early in the season, when there are many hunters in the woods, time is something you just don't have. The longer it takes to get a bird in, the better the chance someone else will interfere.

I do my best to get permission to hunt private lands, as, typically, that is where the best hunting will be. Yet I always seem to spend a few days hunting public land somewhere. I know it will be tough hunting, but I also know that that challenge contributes to an exciting turkey hunt. Pressured gobblers have a way of teaching you everything you need to know about hunting wild turkeys. Many of North America's best turkey hunters learned the ins and outs of this sport by hunting on public land. I tip my hat to those who consistently take turkeys in those areas.

A gobbler will often display his plumage in an open area, where hens have a better chance of seeing him.

The author pauses to listen for distant gobbling. Many times it's best to let the birds talk while you're silent.

When a bird is closing, get set and try to steady your gun on your knee. Your first shot is the one that matters.

The heart-pounding moment of truth has arrived. This hunter must somehow shoulder his gun without being detected.

Always hope that a gobbler will come straight in, but expect him to circle.

The box call is one of the most versatile calls on the market. This hunter is using one in late spring, trying to get the call's raspy sounds to carry in the dense foliage.

Many hunters swear by the slate call. Although it requires the use of two hands, its benefits include producing a wide range of different sounds; it's also good for close-in work.

Some gobblers will walk away from you; when three do, maybe it's time to try some different birds.

These two longbeards have hung up out of range. They are killable, but you have to use the right hunting strategy.

Two hunters working together can draw in a gobbler that otherwise might not come in. Here, the author and his wife, Vikki, discuss strategies.

Locating roost sites can be critical to success. Here, the author examines a turkey feather near a roost.

When a gobbler comes to a call, he will often keep his head high, looking for danger. He'll display if he thinks there is a hen nearby.

Success! The author heads out of the woods with a trophy to be proud of.